FASHION SUPPLY CHAIN AND LOGISTICS MANAGEMENT

The fashion industry has a dynamic, ever-changing landscape. The last decade has seen a shift in consumer expectations and a heightened dependence on efficient and effective supply chain management. These shifts in the consumer mentality have already forced apparel retailers to adapt, making changes throughout their organisations to maintain consumer loyalty. This new text provides an overview of the latest trends and advances in fashion supply chain management and logistics, including:

- The fundamentals of fashion supply chain management
- Strategic management of the fashion supply chain, including the planning aspect of management
- Technology in fashion supply chain management
- Radio-frequency identification (RFID) and interoperability

Drawing on the expertise of academics, researchers and industry experts, including a wealth of real-life international cases, this book is ideal for advanced undergraduate and postgraduate students and academics of fashion management, logistics and supply chain management, as well as practising professionals.

Dr Yi Wang obtained his PhD from the Manufacturing Engineering Centre, Cardiff University, UK, in 2008. He is a lecturer in business decision making in the Faculty of Business, University of Plymouth, UK. Previously he worked in the Department of Computer Science, Southampton University, at the Business School, Nottingham Trent University, and in the School of Materials, University of Manchester. He holds various visiting lectureships in several universities worldwide. Dr Wang has special research interests in supply chain management, logistics, operations management, culture management, information systems, game theory, data analysis, semantics and ontology analysis, and neuromarketing. Dr Wang has published 75 technical peer-reviewed papers in international journals and conferences. He has co-authored two books: *Operations Management for Business* and *Data Mining for Zero-defect Manufacturing*.

'This book provides fundamental information and a valuable resource for the field of fashion supply chain and logistics management. In this book, the author offers a comprehensive overview of many issues related to the fashion industry. Both fashion students and practitioners will find this book of great value.'

Osmud Rahman,
Associate Professor at the School of Fashion,
Ryerson University, Canada

FASHION SUPPLY CHAIN AND LOGISTICS MANAGEMENT

Dr Yi Wang

Routledge
Taylor & Francis Group

LONDON AND NEW YORK

First published 2019
by Routledge
2 Park Square, Milton Park, Abingdon, Oxon OX14 4RN

and by Routledge
711 Third Avenue, New York, NY 10017

Routledge is an imprint of the Taylor & Francis Group, an informa business

© 2019 Yi Wang

The right of Yi Wang to be identified as author of this work has been asserted by him in accordance with sections 77 and 78 of the Copyright, Designs and Patents Act 1988.

All rights reserved. No part of this book may be reprinted or reproduced or utilised in any form or by any electronic, mechanical, or other means, now known or hereafter invented, including photocopying and recording, or in any information storage or retrieval system, without permission in writing from the publishers.

Trademark notice: Product or corporate names may be trademarks or registered trademarks, and are used only for identification and explanation without intent to infringe.

British Library Cataloguing in Publication Data
A catalogue record for this book is available from the British Library

Library of Congress Cataloging-in-Publication Data
Names: Wang, Yi (Lecturer in supply chain management), author.
Title: Fashion supply chain and logistics management / Yi Wang.
Description: Abingdon, Oxon ; New York, NY : Routledge, 2019. | Includes bibliographical references and index.
Identifiers: LCCN 2018030180| ISBN 9781138205536 (hardback : alk. paper) | ISBN 9781138205543 (pbk. : alk. paper) | ISBN 9781315466538 (ebk.)
Subjects: LCSH: Clothing trade. | Business logistics.
Classification: LCC HD9940.A2 W36 2019 | DDC 687.068/7--dc23
LC record available at https://lccn.loc.gov/2018030180

ISBN: 978-1-138-20553-6 (hbk)
ISBN: 978-1-138-20554-3 (pbk)
ISBN: 978-1-315-46653-8 (ebk)

Typeset in Bembo
by Taylor & Francis Books

Printed and bound in Great Britain by
TJ International Ltd, Padstow, Cornwall

CONTENTS

List of tables	*vi*
Foreword	*vii*

1	Basic concepts of the fashion supply chain	1
2	Introduction to fashion	16
3	Lean vs agile supply chain	28
4	Supply chain integration in the apparel industry	44
5	Fashion supply chain traceability: RFID vs barcode	54
6	Consumer behaviour and the fashion supply chain	65
7	Research methodologies for fashion supply chain analysis	75
8	Social media and the fashion supply chain	90
9	The global supply chain risk management	104
10	A delivery system for Sainsbury's clothing brand	115

Index	*127*

TABLES

1.1	Definitions of supply chain	2
1.2	A summary of the main definitions	3
1.3	Strategies used to implement a customer-driven supply chain	5
3.1	Advantages and disadvantages of an agile supply chain	33
3.2	Advantages and disadvantages of a lean supply chain	35
3.3	Similarities and differences of lean and agile supply chains	37
5.1	The choice between RFID and barcodes depends on several factors	60

FOREWORD

The global fashion market was valued at about US$2,400 billion in 2016 and makes 2% of the world's gross domestic product (GDP). It is the seventh largest industry worldwide and is therefore one of the most important in the global economy. On a global scale the fashion industry employed 57.8 million people in 2014. In 2015–2016 the global fashion industry had a growth in sales of 2–2.5%. This growth varied between the different segments and categories. In the European Union (EU) the textile and clothing sector employs 1.7 million people and generates a turnover of €166 billion. About 20% of EU-produced clothes are sold outside the EU. Additionally the EU fashion industry is competitive and trends towards high value-added products. The most important export countries on the other hand are located in Europe. Top countries are Austria with €2,331 billion and the Netherlands with €1,688 billion.

As the global fashion industry becomes more dynamic, fashion companies need to be flexible and agile. Customers are striving for new shopping experiences and more attractive brands. As the industry is growing, well established companies are facing new start-ups that quickly develop into international organisations (e.g. Under Armour, Zalando). All these challenges offer opportunities and risks. New and existing markets need to be thoroughly researched by the companies. To take advantage of these opportunities, companies need to understand the disciplines within the fashion supply chain. This book has been written to provide a comprehensive understanding of current academic research within the fashion industry.

The literature is very precise in describing the challenges of supply chain management, but regarding the specific topics of the fashion industry and fashion retailer, there are few valid sources. This book describes the circumstances of the theories; the relevant scope within the fashion industry is defined by the limitations of practical information. I would like to thank everyone who contributed and supported this book.

1

BASIC CONCEPTS OF THE FASHION SUPPLY CHAIN

1.1 Introduction

The fashion industry has a dynamic, ever-changing landscape. The last decade has seen a shift in consumer expectations and a heightened dependence on supply chain management (Towers et al., 2013; Duclos et al., 2003; Bruce et al., 2004). Consumer trends suggest there will be a wider demand for a higher quality of product, greater transparency within the supply chain, and through increased economic stability consumers will begin to spend more on their apparel products. These shifts in the consumer mentality have already forced apparel retailers to adapt, making changes throughout their organisations to maintain consumer loyalty – an imperative in today's market (Grover & Srinivasan, 1987; Dickson & Ginter, 1987; Krajewski et al., 2005; Teece, 2010).

Furthermore, due to the importance of the supply chain as a point of competitive advantage (Li et al., 2006; Chan et al., 2002), academics and practitioners are predicting a change in the focus of the apparel supply chain such as customisation, lean, agile, flexible and responsive (Melnyk et al., 2010; Reicharhart & Holweg, 2007; Holweg, 2005).

Today, the success of apparel retailers is due to their understanding of two main areas of business: responding to consumer demand and developing products/services that suit the demands of the market. Without a well-developed supply chain, retailers will struggle (Teece, 2010; Porter, 1980). A supply chain will articulate the logic and provide data and other evidence that demonstrates how a business creates and delivers value to consumers (Teece, 2010; Melnyk et al., 2010). The provision of a business determines the basic backbone of the company: target market segment and supply chain management.

Table 1.1 provides a summary of the differing definitions of a supply chain, according to academic publications over the years.

2 Basic concepts

TABLE 1.1 Definitions of supply chain

Reference	Definition
Duclos et al. (2003, p.448)	Encompasses every effort in producing and delivering a final product or service from supplier's supplier to the customers' customer
Chen & Paulraj (2004, p.124–125)	Includes all activities needed to create value: procuring raw materials, converting them into finished goods and offering them to the end customer
Wadhwa et al. (2010, p.150)	A set of interconnected nodes which source, plan, participate, make and deliver different phrases of the value-addition process

All three definitions include some aspect of a process, an interlocking of different activities, leading to a finished product or service. It is these interlocking processes that have to adapt to changing trends in management styles, business models, consumer demands or emerging external factors. A more indepth analysis of some of the ways the demands of the apparel supply chain are shifting will be provided after gaining a greater understanding of a basic apparel supply chain structure.

1.2 Supply chain and supply chain management

Kim et al. (2013) have simplified the reaches of an apparel supply chain to two main areas: supply and retail. There are two main approaches to sourcing products: in-house sourcing and outsourcing. In-house refers to the products and supplies being made by the company themselves (internally), using their own facilities. Outsourcing is the utilisation of an external supplier or partner by the company to make their products. Again the two main approaches to channel strategy are provided: centralised and decentralised.

A centralised strategy means that all key decisions including price, product mix and inventory are tightly controlled by the focal firm. A decentralised approach allows the focal firm to distribute its functions, providing a more agile structure.

Supply chain management (SCM) has become an imperative in today's apparel industry. Table 1.2 provides a summary of the main definitions.

These definitions suggest the management of a supply chain is the ability to integrate all of the processes within a supply chain, seamlessly. The only main difference between the more recent definition and the older definitions is the reference to specific technologies that aid SCM, along with the modern focus on the consumer and their growing influence over the apparel industry.

An apparel retailer's supply chain must maintain consistency with all areas of their company, their corporate strategy and its business environment, including changes enforced by their consumer as well as internal and external issues, problems and

TABLE 1.2 A summary of the main definitions

References	Definition
Duclos et al. (2003, p.448)	Integration of all process within a supply chain into one seamless process. Encompass the processes necessary to create, source, make and deliver
Wadhwa et al. (2010, p.147)	The management of all the below which will increase value in the product through the integration of these supply chain processes
Wadhwa et al. (2010, p.147)	Information technology, rapid and responsive logistics services, effective supplier management and now a higher focus on consumer relationship management

future trends that may threaten profitability (Djelic & Ainamo, 1999). In order to fully achieve consistency all partners of the supply chain need to be efficiently coordinated: vendors, outsourcing partners, distributors, suppliers and consumers (Lee, 2004; Porter, 1986). This consistency will allow retailers to become more effective when adapting to changing market conditions such as those suggested above (Christopher et al., 2004; Masson et al., 2007).

Academics have understood the importance of SCM in coordinating amongst all aspects of the supply chain ever since the focus moved from retailers driving the industry to the consumer gaining greater influence (Cousins, 2005; Teece, 2010). In order to fulfil customers' requirements companies have had to focus their resources on the efficient management of their supply chains (Schiele, 2006; Cousins, 2005; Towers et al., 2013). Since this shift it has become arguable that the SCM holds a greater role within an apparel company than any other organisational function, especially when addressing social and environmental responsibility (Tate et al., 2010), a consumer trend of increasing importance (Bendell & Kleanthous, 2007).

With an increase in the complexity of today's supply chain, through the competitive environment becoming international, more dynamic and customer driven, there is an ever-increasing need for firms to look beyond their own borders and manage their entire system, processes and activities (Duclos et al., 2003). Manufacturers cannot maintain large volume production while balancing cost efficiency with increasing levels of change and uncertainty. A need arose to align their supply chain partners with a common set of goals to ensure all elements are focused on the impeding supply chain demands: flexibility, speed and cost (Wimer, 2001).

With the focus on optimising core activities, maximising speed of response to changing consumer demands (Chase et al., 2000), reducing lead times and improving efficiency, there is an increasing need for a responsive approach to SCM (Bruce et al., 2004). Moreover, firms have begun to look further into areas of delivery, flexibility and innovation in order to develop competitive advantage (Duclos et al., 2003). All of these areas of increasing focus have one generalisation between them: the aspect of time. It has been said that one way to achieve this responsiveness is through SCM (Duclos et al., 2003).

4 Basic concepts

1.3 Supply chain environment

The contemporary business environment is subject to intense competition and dynamic environmental changes: short product life cycles, changing demand pattern, dynamic market, presence of multiple competitors, customer demand for personalised products (Wadhwa et al., 2010), mass customisation of product, and increased variety of products (Chase et al., 2000; Reicharhart & Holweg, 2007), better service, increased reliability and faster delivery (Duclos et al., 2003). Each of these changes is shaping the apparel supply chain of today in many ways; strategies to increase flexibility and quick response are being implemented throughout the apparel industry.

The increased sophistication of consumers means they have a higher expectation of the performance of apparel supply chains. Retailers are finding ways to revitalise their manufacturing capabilities to provide consumers with better products, faster, with a lower cost, personalised, ethically made and environmentally friendly (Rollins et al., 2003).

The contemporary apparel market has to compete in terms of time, cost, quality and the flexibility of their supply chains, resulting in a shift from cost-critical to time-critical manufacturing (Rollins et al., 2003). In response to this shift in focus, retailers have implemented customer-driven supply chains. Academic literature suggests three main types of customer-driven supply chain: build-to-order (BTO), just-in-time (JIT), and postponement. Table 1.3 provides a summary of the main advantages they provide an apparel retailer.

Wadhwa et al. (2010) have suggested three major problems facing the global supply chain:

- A lack of communication and cooperation within the supply chain
- Unnecessary complexity – too many players in the global supply chain, from raw material suppliers to retail sales channels
- Customer requirements are changing fast – difficult to achieve a level of responsiveness from this complexity.

1.4 Outsourcing and off-shoring

Rollins et al. (2003) focus on the impending problems that come with the outsourcing of many manufacturing functions. These functions have, in majority, been outsourced to areas of the world such as Asia, Africa and the Middle East. Due to the increase in manufacturing capabilities and sourcing industries developing in these areas of the world, these economies are beginning to grow substantially. In terms of growth the UK is located fourth with $1.6 trillion in 2002, predicted to move to fifth in 2019 with $3.8 trillion. In reference to developing countries they are not present in the 2002 top ten world economies in terms of size; however, this

Basic concepts 5

TABLE 1.3 Strategies used to implement a customer-driven supply chain

Supply chain type	Definition	Advantages
Build-to order (BTO)	The manufacture of products or services based on the requirements of an individual customer or a group of customers at competitive prices and within a short time span (Gunasekaran & Ngai, 2005, p.425)	• Fast, reliable, customised (Gunasekaran & Ngai, 2005; Holweg & Pil, 2001) • More effective matching of product to customer need; enhancing satisfaction and loyalty (Sharma & LaPlaca, 2005) • Enables cost saving; reduces raw materials, space; and increases flexibility (Agarwal et al., 2001)
Just-in-time (JIT)	Focuses on purchasing and manufacturing items which belong to the products for immediate consumption (Ho & Kao, 2013, p.751)	• Improves customer service and inventory turnover (Achabal et al., 2000) • Improves product quality and reduces waste from the production system (Ho & Kao, 2013)
Postponement	The postponement of specification decisions in the production process to reduce initial product variety (Reicharhart & Holweg, 2007, p.1159)	• Delays value addition until demand is visible (Wadhwa et al., 2010) • Improves supply chain leanness (Zinn & Bowersox, 1988) • Mitigates risk (Aviv, 2001) • Promotes flexibility to satisfy the needs of product variety and quick response (Lee et al., 1993)

changes as time goes on. In 2014 India stands tenth with $2 trillion and is expected to grow further to occupy seventh position in 2019 with $3.1 trillion.

Even though economic size indicates impressive growth for India in particular, in general, the figures are dominated by developing countries. The difference comes when looking closely at the areas within which these countries reside. There is a positive relationship between the countries that enjoy the most economic growth in 2014 and the areas within which apparel manufacturing processes have been outsourced: Bangladesh (7.0%), India (6.8%), Nigeria (6.7%), China (6.5%), Indonesia (6%) and the Philippines (6%). The outsourcing of apparel manufacture may not be the sole or most significant factor in the development of these economies, but it has certainly had an impact.

There are many major impacts this economic growth has had, on both the countries in question themselves, but also on the apparel industry. The improved sophistication, reliability and global communications of these countries have led to a reduction in cost competition and an increase in logistical obstacles for leading high street retailers (ILO, 2014/15). This increase in wages will make it significantly more difficult for the dominant high street retailers to maintain their competitive advantage, in terms of cost. The main advantage of moving manufacture off-shore was to maintain lower costs within manufacture and move this

6 Basic concepts

saving through direct to the consumer. This strategy is now becoming questionable.

The final problem facing today's apparel supply chain, according to Rollins et al. (2003), refers to today's manufacturing of garments not being suited to the mass-production techniques needed to provide low-cost apparel. This is due to the short life cycles of products and the regular changes in item configuration and materials used for each product (OECD, 2015). High production equipment is costly, difficult to use and uneconomical, which means that mass production remains dependent on the expertise and skill of the workforce assigned to manufacturing roles.

The outsourcing of production phases to complex networks of partners off-shore (Caridi et al., 2013) has impacted Europe in a huge way: 50,000 jobs were lost in the UK in the ten years to 1994, and 280,000 were lost in total throughout Europe (European Union, 1994).

The main reason the apparel industry turned to outsourcing is due to the significant difference in the wages provided to workers elsewhere in the world: £1 per hour or less (Brazil, China, India, etc.), compared to under £6 per hour in the UK (Rollins et al., 2003; *Business Insider*, 2013). Consequently, the cost of manufacturing is dramatically reduced, enabling retailers to relocate this saving directly to the consumer.

This new trend within the apparel industry to go global, sourcing and manufacturing off-shore (Stratton & Warburton, 2006), has caused rapid change in the nature of competition and the degree of risk exposure felt by the industry (Tang & Musa, 2011; Doeringer & Courault, 2008). Off-shoring has introduced many new challenges to the industry: unforeseen risks in the delivery process, rigid negotiability, language barriers and international business customs which need to be overcome in order to deliver a high level of service to the end consumer (Towers & Song, 2010). These risks have substantially increased the hostility of the environment (Kilduff, 2000), introducing fierce competition throughout (Newman & Cullen, 2002).

In order for apparel companies to cope with these challenges they have been forced to focus their core competences, externalising even more of their activities to other firms. This externalisation has resulted in vast, complex and intricate supply chains; even finished products are delivered worldwide through increasingly complex distribution networks (Caridi et al., 2013). As a direct result from off-shoring, modern competition has shifted from company vs company to supply chain vs supply chain (Li et al., 2006; Chan et al., 2002; Cox, 1999; Christopher, 1998). It is for this reason that this chapter has focused on the principles of the apparel supply chain, in a bid to provide stable arguments for the relocation of manufacturing processes back on-shore.

1.5 Fast fashion

Another industry trend that emerged hand in hand with the move off-shore is 'fast fashion', characterised by marketing factors such as low predictability, high-impulse purchase, shorter life cycles and high volatility of market demand (Fernie & Sparks, 1998).

Some of the changing dynamics of the fashion industry were outcomes from the move to outsourcing: mass production, an increase in the number of fashion seasons and a change in the structural characteristics of the supply chain. These changes forced retailers to focus on low cost and flexibility in design, quality, delivery and speed to market (Doyle et al., 2006). The focus on speed to market (reducing the time gap between design and consumption on a seasonal basis), and providing fashion trends to the end consumer rapidly, are the origins of fast fashion (Taplin, 1999).

In order to have success here it is imperative to gain market agility, and therefore responsiveness, through the incorporation of consumer preferences to the design process (Christopher et al., 2004). One example of this is the consumer demand for retailers to 'refresh' their product ranges. Retailers are expected to increase the variety of their designs and on a more regular basis, increasing the number of seasons and introducing the idea of 'Here Today, Gone Tomorrow' (Bhardwaj & Fairhurst, 2010). As a direct result of this mentality, and of the fast fashion trend in general creating short product life cycles due to the sale of fast-selling merchandise (Sydney, 2008), apparel consumers of today have become part of a 'throwaway market' (Tokatli, 2008).

Fast fashion may have developed into the standard strategic model for the majority, if not all retailers on the high street. However, there is an increasing juxtaposition in the fast fashion industry between low-cost, high-volume manufacture, and customer responsiveness in such a dynamic marketplace (Brindley & Oxborrow, 2014; Barnes & Lea-Greenwood, 2006). The importance of getting this balance correct has never been higher due to the increasing power of the consumer (Brindley & Oxborrow, 2014).

Businesses have to become more consumer-centric (Teece, 2010). This focus has resulted in the common agreement that consumer demand, actual or forecasted, activates the daily flow within supply chains (customer driven), instead of the supplier of the product or service being the driving force behind daily supply chain activities (supply driven) (Hull, 2005).

Recent consumer research has established many new trends that will play a part in the future of fashion retail, some of which include: the importance of sustainability (Towers et al., 2013; Kozar et al., 2013; Bendell & Kleanthous, 2007), negative attitudes to quality decline (Goworek et al., 2012; Chau, 2012; Morgan & Birtwistle, 2009; Birtwistle & Moore, 2007), willingness to pay for ethical products (Mai, 2014; Ellis et al., 2012; Hustvedt & Dickson, 2009), a reversion to older ways of shopping (Deloitte Consumer Tracker, 2018; Drapers, 2014), and mass customisation (Senanayake & Little, 2010; Silveira et al., 2001).

1.6 Sustainable supply and logistics

One of the main consumer trends of today's apparel industry is that of sustainability (Deloitte Consumer Tracker, 2018). Sustainability issues have only one main solution: higher supply chain transparency (SCT). SCT is defined as the continuing

8 Basic concepts

commitment by businesses to behave ethically and contribute to economic development, while improving the quality of life of the workforce and their families as well as of the local community and society (WBCSD, 1999). SCT can be further separated into two main areas when specifically referencing the apparel industry: environmental responsibility (issues of pollution and depletion of natural resources), and social responsibility (issues of wages, working hours and conditions) (Towers et al., 2013).

It is becoming increasingly noted that not only do retailers have to change the ways in which they carry out their business, but also consumers need to be educated in a bid to sway their purchasing habits in a more ethical direction (Kozar & Hiller Connell, 2010; Dickson et al., 2009; Carrigan & Attalla, 2001; Dickson, 1999). In an American study, Kim et al. (1999) found a positive relationship between consumers' attitudes towards social and environmental responsibilities and their intentions to purchase from socially responsible companies.

Even though it seems there are many initiatives and movements towards the reduction of sustainability issues within the apparel industry, there are still some obstacles that must be overcome. For example, the majority of consumers have perceptions that ethical products are of a higher price, few firms actually offer socially and environmentally responsible products (Hiller Connell, 2010), and consumers do not want to be inconvenienced when they do intend to purchase ethically (Carrigan & Attalla, 2001). Hiller Connell (2010) suggests that more resources, in terms of time and effort, are required if ethical companies are to be favoured by the consumer. Carrigan and Attalla (2001) propose that consumers must be convinced that a change in their purchasing habits will make a significant difference, echoing the call for thorough, in-depth and focused education, engagement and awareness of the issues surrounding social and environmental responsibility.

Ethical consumers represent a growing market segment (Shaw & Tomolillo, 2004), typically young, female, well-educated urban dwellers (Laroche et al., 2001; Banerjee & McKeage, 1994; Arbuthnot, 1977; Weigel, 1977). Third-party accreditation is an assurance to consumers (Kirchhoff, 2000; McCluskey, 2000) that marketing attributes of quality are in fact well founded (Mai, 2014).

When purchasing products of an ethical origin, consumers are driven by factors such as quality and value, resulting in a willingness to pay (WTP) more for ethical products (Mai, 2014). WTP is an economic concept, defined as the amount a person is willing to give up to be indifferent between having and not having the good (Ellis et al., 2012, p.291). Studies undertaken by Ellis et al. (2012), and Hustvedt and Dickson (2009) found that consumers thought of ethical products as better quality (found to be a significant variable), resulting in a willingness to pay more for ethical products.

Finally, studies into the ethical consumer suggest consumer self-identity is another variable linked to socially and environmentally responsible consumers (Hustvedt & Dickson, 2009). Self-identity is defined as the relatively enduring characteristics that people ascribe to themselves, often synonymous with self-perception or self-concept (Sparks & Guthrie, 1998, p.1396). The self-identification as a green consumer is suggested to have an impact on their behaviour as well as their attitude towards ethical products and their moral obligation to purchase these products (Hustvedt & Dickson, 2009; Stets & Biga, 2003; Shaw et al., 2000; Sparks & Shepherd, 1992).

In previous years the main focus of the apparel industry has been to optimise cost structure, impacting every area of the supply chain in addition to brand strategies and values (Rollins et al., 2003). However, this is no longer the only competitive factor; consumers are becoming increasingly upset with the level of decreasing quality provided by apparel retailers. Low product quality is one major reason why consumers stop wearing cheap clothing (Birtwistle & Moore, 2007; Morgan & Birtwistle, 2009). Goworek et al. (2012) suggest that garments of cheap material are of poor quality, thrown away after one or two uses only (Chau, 2012); sometimes this is not due to consumer choice: garments fall apart after a single wear (Joung, 2014).

The Deloitte Consumer Tracker (2018) shows the highest level of consumer confidence since the tracker began in 2011. There is more optimism surrounding issues such as 'levels of disposable income' and 'levels of debt', and the improving labour market has helped overall confidence: fewer people are experiencing 'loss or reduction of income' or 'being made redundant / losing jobs'. More specifically the demographic of 18–34 year olds are said to be feeling more confident about future prospects than their older counterparts.

As an effect of increasing reliability of their financial situation consumers are reverting to older ways and principles of shopping (*Drapers*, 2014). The year 2008 marked the beginning of the economic downturn in the UK, during which price took over as the main driver of purchase decisions. The years 2010–2012 have shown an increase in the amount of disposable income available to consumers, meaning that consumers are now able to return to their older principles of shopping, demanding higher-quality products. It has been suggested by *Drapers* (2014) that these changes are likely to be permanent, reversing the price war that took over the high street during the economic downturn.

In order to provide a fuller, in-depth understanding of the term Fashion, it is also important to study the entrance of a customer into the product life cycle, and its effect on the finished product (Wortmann, 1997; Lampel & Mintzberg, 1996; Senanayake & Little, 2010). This involvement of the consumer in the product life cycle has many similarities to the hybrid manufacturing models used by New Look, H&M and Primark, and theories relating to customisation.

References

Achabal, D.D., Mchintyre, S.H., Smith, S.A. & Kalyanam, K. (2000). A decision support system for vendor managed inventory. *Journal of Retailing*, 76(4), pp. 430–454.

Agarwal, M., Kumaresh, T.V. & Mercer, G.A. (2001). The false promise of mass customization. *McKinsey Quarterly*, 3, pp. 62–71.

Arbuthnot, J. (1977). The roles of attitudinal and personality variables in the prediction of environmental behaviour and knowledge. *Environment and Behaviour*, 9(2), pp. 217–232.

10 Basic concepts

Aviv, Y. (2001). The effect of collaborative forecasting on supply chain performance. *Management Science*, 47(10), pp. 1326–1343.

Banerjee, B. & McKeage, K. (1994). 'How green is my value: Exploring the relationship between environmentalism and materialism', in C.T. Allen & D.R. John (eds), *Advances in Consumer Research*. Provo, UT: Association for Consumer Research, Vol. 21, pp. 147–152.

Barnes, L. & Lea-Greenwood, G. (2006). Fast fashioning the supply chain: Shaping the research agenda. *Journal of Fashion Marketing and Management*, 10(3), pp. 259–271.

Bendell, J. & Kleanthous, A. (2007). Deeper luxury: Quality and style when the world matters. Available at: www.wwf.org.uk/deeperluxury/ [accessed December 2017].

Bhardwaj, V. & Fairhurst, A. (2010). Fast fashion: Response to changes in the fashion industry. *The International Review of Retail, Distribution and Consumer Research*, 20(1), pp. 165–173.

Birtwistle, G. & Moore, C.M. (2007). Fashion Clothing – Where does it all end up? *International Journal of Retail & Distribution Management*, 35(3), pp. 210–216.

Blome, C., Schoenherr, T. & Rexhausen, D. (2013). Antecedents and enablers of supply chain agility and its effect on performance: A dynamic capabilities perspective. *International Journal of Production Research*, 51(4), pp. 1295–1318.

Bower, J.L. & Hout, T.M. (1988). Fast-cycle Capability for Competitive Power. *Harvard Business Review*, 66(6), pp. 110–188.

Brainard, S.L. & Riker, D.A. (1997). *Are US Multinationals Exporting US Jobs?*NBER Working Paper, No. 5958. Cambridge, MA. Available at: www.nber.org/papers/w5958.pdf.

Brindley, C. & Oxborrow, L. (2014). Aligning the sustainable supply chain to green marketing needs: A case study. *Industrial Marketing Management*, 43(1), January, pp. 45–55.

Bruce, M., Daly, M. & Towers, N. (2004). Lean or agile: A solution for supply chain management in the textiles and clothing industry? *International Journal of Operations & Production Management*, 24(2), pp. 151–170.

Burgess, R.G. (1982). *Field Research: A Source Book and Field Manual*. London: Allen and Unwin (2nd edn, Routledge, 1991).

Business Insider (2013). Here's how America's Minimum Wage Stacks up Against Countries Like India, Russia, Greece and France. Available at: www.businessinsider.com/a-look-at-minimum-wagesaround-the-world-2013-8 [accessed 4 July 2014].

Caridi, M., Perego, A. & Tunino, A. (2013). Measuring Supply Chain Visibility in the Apparel Industry. *Benchmarking: An International Journal*, 20(1), pp. 25–44.

Carrigan, M. & Attalla, A. (2001). The Myth of the Ethical Consumer – Do Ethics Matter in Purchase Behaviour? *Journal of Consumer Marketing*, 18(7), pp. 560–577.

Catalan, M. & Kotzab, H. (2003). Assessing the Responsiveness in the Danish Mobile Phone Supply Chain. *International Journal of Physical Distribution & Logistics Management*, 33(8), pp. 668–685.

Chan, F.T.S., Nelson, K.H., Tang, H.C.W., & Lau, R.W.L. (2002). A simulation approach in supply chain management. *Integrated Manufacturing Systems*, 13(2), pp. 117–122.

Charmaz, K. (1983). 'The Grounded Theory Method: An Explication and Interpretation', in R. Emerson (ed.), *Contemporary Field Research*. Boston: Little Brown.

Chase, R.B., Aquilano, N.J. & Jacobs, R. (2000). *Operations Management of Competitive Advantage*. Boston, MA: Irwin/McGraw-Hill.

Chau, L. (2012). The Wasteful Culture of Forever 21, H&M, and Fast Fashion. Available at: www.usnews.com/opinion/blogs/economicintelligence/ 2012/09/21/the-wasteful-culture-of-forever 21-hm-and-fastfashion.

Chen, I. & Paulraj, A. (2004). Towards a Theory of Supply Chain Management: The constructs and measurements. *Journal of Operations Management*, 22, pp. 119–150.

Childerhouse, P. & Towill, D. (2000). Engineering supply chains to match customer requirements. *Logistics Information Management*, 13(6), pp. 337–346.

Christopher, M. (1998). Logistics and Competitive Strategy. *Logistics Information Management*, 1(4), pp. 204–206.

Christopher, M., Lowson, R. & Peck, H. (2004). Creating agile supply chains in the fashion industry. *International Journal of Retail & Distribution Management*, 32(8), pp. 367–376.

Cousins, J.B. (2005). 'Will the real empowerment evaluation please stand up? A critical friend perspective', in D. Fetterman & A. Wandersman (eds), *Empowerment evaluation principles in practice*. New York: Guilford, pp. 183–208.

Cox, A. (1999). Power, value and supply chain management. *Supply Chain Management: An International Journal*, 4(4), pp. 167–175.

Da Silveira, G., Borenstein, D. & Fogliatto, F.S. (2001). Mass customization: Literature review and research directions. *International Journal of Production Economics*, 72(1), pp. 1–13.

Deloitte Consumer Tracker (2018). *Confidence on the up as consumers defy expectations*. Available at: www2.deloitte.com/content/dam/Deloitte/uk/Documents/consumer-business/deloitte-uk-consumer-tracker-q2-2018.pdf [accessed April 2018].

Dickson, M.A. (1999). US consumers' knowledge of and concern with apparel sweatshops. *Journal of Fashion Marketing and Management: An International Journal*, 3(1), pp. 44–55.

Dickson, M.A., Loker, S. & Eckman, M. (2009). *Social responsibility in the global apparel industry*. New York, NY: Fairchild Books.

Dickson, P.R. & Ginter, J. (1987). Market Segmentation, Product Differentiation, and Marketing Strategy. *Journal of Marketing*, 5(2), pp. 1–10.

Djelic, M.-L. & Ainamo, A. (1999). The coevolution of new organization forms in the fashion industry: A historical and comparative study of France, Italy and the United States. *Organization Science*, 10, pp. 622–637.

Doeringer, P. & Courault, B. (2008). Garment District Performance: Sweatshop efficiency vs Innovation efficiency. *Alfred P. Sloan Foundation Industry Studies, Annual Conference Proceedings*, May.

Doyle, S.A., Moore, C.M. & Morgan, L. (2006). Supplier Management in Fast Moving Fashion Retailing. *Journal of Fashion Marketing and Management*, 10(3), pp. 272–281.

Drapers (2013). We Must be Careful to Define what 'Made in Britain' Means, 26 July. Available at: www.drapersonline.com/comment/talking-business/we-must-becareful-to-define-what-made-in-britain-means/5051427.article#.U48ZssU_ IU [accessed 4 July 2014].

Drapers (2014). Are Consumers Reverting Back to the Old Ways of Shopping?, 1 May. Available at: www.drapersonline.com/5059906.article?WT.tsrc=email&WT.mc_id=Newsletter182#.U4y1H8sU_IV [accessed 4 July 2014].

Du, L. (2007). Acquiring Competitive Advantage in Industry through Supply Chain Integration: A Case Study of Yue Yuen Industrial Holdings Ltd. *Journal of Enterprise Information Management*, 20(5), pp. 527–543.

Duclos, L.K., Vokurka, R.J. & Lummus, R.R. (2003). A Conceptual Model of Supply Chain Flexibility. *Industrial Management and Data Systems*, 103(6), pp. 446–456.

Egger, H. & Egger, P. (2003). Outsourcing and Skill-specific Employment in a Small Economy: Austria after the fall of the Iron Curtain. *Oxford Economic Papers*, 55(4), pp. 625–643.

Ellis, J.L., McCracken, V.A. & Skuza, N. (2012). Insights into willingness to pay for organic cotton apparel. *Journal of Fashion Marketing and Management*, 16(3), pp. 290–305.

Esterby-Smith, M., Thorpe, R. & Lowe, A. (2002). *Management Research: An Introduction.* London: Sage Publications.

European Union (1994). *Eurostats OETH DEBA, E.U.* Commission Eurostats E.U Comitextil: textilwirtchaft: Dable.

Fernie, J. & Sparks, L. (1998). *Logistics and Retail Management: Insights into Current Practice and Trends from Leading Experts.* London: Kogan Page.

Field, A. (2009). *Discovering Statistics: Using SPSS.* London: Sage.

Fine, C. (2013). Intelli-sourcing to Replace Off-shoring as Supply Chain Transparency Increases. *Journal of Supply Chain Management,* 49(2), pp. 6–7.

Fisher, M.L., Hammond, J.H., Obermeyer, W.R. & Raman, A. (1994). Making Supply Meet Demand in an Uncertain World. *Harvard Business Review,* 72(3), pp. 83–93.

Forrester, J.W. (1961). *Industrial Dynamics.* Cambridge, MA: MIT Press.

Gilmore, J.H. & Pine, B.J. (1997). The Four Faces of Mass Customization. *Harvard Business Review,* 75(1), pp. 91–101.

Glaser, B.B.G. & Strauss, A.L. (1967). *The Discovery of Grounded Theory: Strategies for Qualitative Research.* New York: Aldine.

Goldman, S.L. & Nagel, R.N. (1993). Management, Technology and Agility: The emergence of a new era in manufacturing. *International Journal of Technology Management,* 8(1/2), pp. 18–38.

Goworek, H., Fosher, T., Copper, T., Woodward, S. & Hiller, A. (2012). The Sustainable Clothing Market: An Evaluation of Potential Strategies for UK Retailers. *International Journal of Retail & Distribution Management,* 40(12), pp. 935–955.

Grover, R. & Srinivasan, V. (1987). A Simultaneous Approach to Market Segmentation and Market Structuring. *Journal of Marketing Research,* 24 (May), pp. 139–153.

Gunasekaran, A. & Ngai, E.W.T. (2005). Build-to-Order Supply Chain Management: A Literature Review and Framework for Development. *Journal of Operations Management,* 23 (5), pp. 423–451.

Habermas, J. (1970). 'Knowledge and Interest', in D. Emmett & A. Macintyre (eds), *Sociological Theory and Philosophical Analysis.* London: Macmillan.

Hammer, M. (1990). Re-engineering Work: Don't Automate Obliterate. *Harvard Business Review,* 68(4) (July–August), pp. 104–109.

Harris, L.M. (1996). Expanding Horizons. *Marketing Research: A Magazine of Management and Application,* 8(2) (Summer), p. 12.

Hiller Connell, K.Y. (2010). Internal and External Barriers to Eco-conscious Apparel Acquisition. *International Journal of Consumer Studies,* 34(3), pp. 279–286.

Hines, P. (1998). Benchmarking Toyota's Supply Chain: Japan vs. UK. *Long Range Planning,* 31(6), pp. 911–918.

Hines, P., Holweg, M. & Rich, N. (2004). Learning to Evolve: A Review of Contemporary Lean Thinking. *International Journal of Operations and Production Management,* 24(10), pp. 994–1011.

Hines, T. (2004). *Supply Chain Strategies: Customer-driven and Customer Focused.* Oxford: Elsevier Butterworth-Heinemann.

Hines, T. & McGowan, P. (2005). Supply Chain Strategies in the UK Fashion Industry: The Rhetoric of Partnership and Realities of Power. *International Entrepreneurship and Management Journal,* 1(4), pp. 519–537.

Hirst, P. & Zeitlin, J. (1990). *Reversing Industrial Decline.* Oxford: Basil Blackwell.

Ho, L.H. & Kao, W.F. (2013). Applying a Just-in-Time Integrated Supply Chain Model with Inventory and Waste Reduction Considerations. *Am. J. Applied Sci.,* 10, pp. 751–759.

Holweg, M. (2005). An Investigation into Supplier Responsiveness: Empirical Evidence from the Automotive Industry. *International Journal of Logistics Management,* 16(1), pp. 96–119.

Holweg, M. & Pil, F.K. (2001). Successful Build-to-Order Strategies Start with the Customer. *MIT Sloan Management Review*, 43(1), pp. 74–83.

Hull, B.Z. (2005). Are Supply (Driven) Chains Forgotten? *The International Journal of Logistics Management*, 16(16), pp. 218–236.

Husic, M. & Cicic, M. (2009). Luxury Consumption Factors. *Journal of Fashion Marketing and Management*, 13(2), pp. 231–245.

Hustvedt, G. & Dickson, M.A. (2009). Consumer Likelihood of Purchasing Organic Cotton Apparel: Influence of Attitudes and Self-identity. *Journal of Fashion Marketing and Management*, 13(1), pp. 49–65.

International Labour Organization (ILO) (2014/15). *Global Wage Report 2014/15*. Available at: www.ilo.org/global/about-the-ilo/multimedia/maps-andcharts/ WCMS_193294/la ng-en/index.htm [accessed 4 July 2014].

Jahns, C., Hartmann, E. & Bals, L. (2006). Off-shoring: Dimensions and Diffusion of a New Business Concept. *Journal of Purchasing & Supply Management*, 12(4), pp. 218–231.

Jones, S. (1987). 'Choosing Action Research: A Rationale', in I.L. Mangham (ed.), *Organisation Analysis and Development*. Chichester: Wiley.

Joung, H.M. (2014). Fast Fashion Consumers' Post-Purchase Behaviours. *International Journal of Retail and Distribution Management*, 42(8), pp. 688–697.

Kehoe, D.F., Boughton, N.J. & Sharifi, H. (2001). Demand Network Alignment: An Empirical View. The UK Symposium on Supply Chain Alignment, Liverpool, July.

Kilduff, P. (2000). Evolving Strategies, Structures and Relationships in Complex and Turbulent Business Environments: The Textile and Apparel Industries of the New Millennium. *Journal of Textile and Apparel, Technology and Management*, 1(1), pp. 1–9.

Kim, H., Choo, H.J. & Yoon, N. (2013). The motivational drivers of fast fashion avoidance. *Journal of Fashion Marketing and Management: An International Journal*, 17(2), pp. 243–260.

Kim, N., Bridges, E. & Srivastava, R.K. (1999). A simulation model for innovative product category sales diffusion and competitive dynamic. *International Journal of Research in Marketing*, 16, pp. 95–111.

Kirchhoff, S. (2000). Green Business and Blue Angels: A Model of Voluntary Over Compliance with Asymmetric Information. *Environmental and Resource Economics*, 15(4), pp. 403–420.

Kozar, J.M. & Hiller Connell, K.Y. (2010). Socially responsible knowledge and behaviors: Comparing upper- vs lower-classmen. *College Student Journal*, 44(2), pp. 279–293.

Kozar, J.M. & Hiller Connell, K.Y. (2013). Socially and environmentally responsible apparel consumption: Knowledge, attitudes, and behaviors. *Social Responsibility Journal*, 9(2), pp. 315–324.

Krajewski, L., Wei, J.C. & Tang, L.-L. (2005). Responding to schedule changes in build-to-order supply chains. *Journal of Operations Management*, 23, pp. 451–469.

Lampel, J. & Mintzberg, H. (1996). Customizing customisation. *Sloan Management Review*, 38(1), pp. 21–30.

Laroche, M., Bergeron, J. & Barbaro-Forleo, G. (2001). Targeting Consumers Who are Willing to Pay more for Environmentally-Friendly Products. *Journal of Consumer Marketing*, 18(6), pp. 503–520.

Latour, B. & Woolgar, S. (1979). *Laboratory Life: The Social Construction of Scientific Facts*. Beverly Hills: Sage.

Lau, R.S.M. (1994). *Attaining Strategic Flexibility*. Paper presented at the 5th Annual Meeting of the Production and Operations Management Society, 8–11 October, Washington, DC.

Lee, H.L. (2004). Creating Value through Supply Chain Integration. *Supply Chain Management Review*, 4(4), pp. 30–36.

14 Basic concepts

Lee, H.L., Billington, C. & Carter, B. (1993). Hewlett-Packard Gains Control of Inventory and Service through Design for Localization. *Interfaces*, 23(4), pp. 1–11.

Li, S., Ragu-Nathan, B., Ragu-Nathan, T. & Rao, S. (2006). The impact of supply chain management practices on competitive advantage and organizational performance. *Omega*, 34(2), pp. 107–124.

Lincoln, Y. & Denzin, N. (2003). *Strategies of Qualitative Inquiry*. Sage.

MacDuffie, J.P., Sethuraman, K. & Fisher, M.L. (1996). Product Variety and Manufacturing Performance: Evidence from the International Assembly Plant Study. *Management Science*, 42(3), pp. 350–369.

Mai, L.W. (2014). Consumers' willingness to pay for ethical attributes. *Marketing Intelligence & Planning*, 32(6), pp. 706–721.

Masson, R. et al. (2007). Managing complexity in agile global fashion industry supply chains. *The International Journal of Logistics Management*, 18(2), pp. 238–254.

McCluskey, J.J. (2000). A Game Theoretic Approach to Organic Foods: An Analysis of Asymmetric Information and Policy. *Agricultural and Resource Economics*, 29(1), pp. 1–9.

Melnyk, S.A., Davis, E.W., Spekman, R.E. & Sandor, J. (2010). Outcome-Driven Supply Chains. *MIT Sloan Management Review*, Winter, 51(2), pp. 33–338.

Morgan, L.R. & Birtwistle, G. (2009). An investigation of young fashion consumers' disposal habits. *International Journal of Consumer Studies*, 33, pp. 190–198.

Newman, A.J. & Cullen, P. (2002). *Retailing: Environment & operations*. London: Thomson.

Organisation for Economic Co-operation and Development (OECD) (2015). *OECD Innovation Strategy 2015: An Agenda for Policy Action*. Paris: OECD Publishing.

Porter, M.E. (1980). *Competitive Strategy*. New York: The Free Press.

Porter, M., ed. (1986). *Competition in Global Industries*. Boston, MA: Harvard Business School Press, pp. 19, 24.

Reicharhart, A. & Holweg, M. (2007). Creating the customer-responsive supply chain: A reconciliation of concepts. *International Journal of Operations & Production Management*, 27 (11), pp. 1144–1172.

Rollins, R.P., Porter, K. & Little, D. (2003). Modelling the changing apparel supply chain. *International Journal of Clothing Science and Technology*, 15(2), pp. 140–156.

Schiele, H. (2006). *Quantifying the impact of the purchasing function's sophistication on cost savings through balanced sourcing strategies*. Paper presented at the IMP Conference, Milan, Italy. Available at: www.impgroup.org/uploads/papers/5789.pdf [accessed February 2018].

Senanayake, M.M. & Little, J.T. (2010). Mass customization: Points and extent of apparel customization. *Journal of Fashion Marketing and Management*, 14(2), pp. 282–299.

Sharma, A. & LaPlaca, P. (2005). Marketing in the emerging era of build-to order manufacturing. *Industrial Marketing Management*, 34(5), pp. 476–486.

Shaw, D., Shiu, E. & Clarke, I. (2000). The Contribution of Ethical Obligation and Self-Identity to the Theory of Planned Behaviour: An Exploration of Ethical Consumers. *Journal of Marketing Management*, 16(8), pp. 879–894.

Shaw, D. & Tomolillo, D.A.C. (2004). 'Undressing the ethical issues in fashion: A consumer perspective', in M. Bruce, C. Moore & G. Birtwistle (eds), *International Retail Marketing*. Oxford: Butterworth-Heinemann, pp. 141–152.

Sparks, P. & Guthrie, C.A. (1998). Self-identity and the theory of planned behavior: A useful addition or an unhelpful artifice? *Journal of Applied Social Psychology*, 28, pp. 1393–1410.

Sparks, P. & Shepherd, R. (1992). Self-identity and the Theory of Planned Behavior: Assessing the Role of Identification with 'Green Consumerism'. *Social Psychology Quarterly*, 55(4), pp. 388–399.

Stets, J.E. & Biga, C.F. (2003). Bringing Identity Theory into Environmental Sociology. *Sociological Theory*, 21, pp. 398–423.

Stratton, R. & Warburton, R. (2006). Managing the trade-off implications of global supply. *International Journal of Production Economics*, 103, pp. 667–679.

Suhong, Li, Ragu-Nathan, B., Ragu-Nathan, T.S. & Subba Rao, S. (2006). The Impact of Supply Chain Management Practices on Competitive Advantage and Organizational Performance. *Omega*, 34(2), pp. 107–124.

Sydney (2008). *Fast fashion is not a trend*. Available at: www.sydneylovesfashion.com/2008/12/fast-fashion-is-trend.html [accessed 20 September 2017].

Tang, O. & Musa, S.N. (2011). Identifying risk issues and research advancements in supply chain risk management. *International Journal of Production Economics*, 133, pp. 25–34.

Taplin, I.M. (1999). Continuity and change in the US apparel industry: A statistical profile. *Journal of Fashion Marketing and Management*, 3(4), pp. 360–368.

Tate, A., Chen-Burger, Y.-H., Dalton, J., Potter, S., Richardson, D., Stader, J. & Williams, P.G. (2010). A Virtual Space for Intelligent Interaction. *IEEE Intelligent Systems*, July/August, pp. 62–71.

Teece, J.T. (2010). Business models, business strategy, and innovation. *Long Range Plan*, 43, pp. 172–194.

Tokatli, N. (2008). Global sourcing: Insights from the global clothing industry – the case of Zara, a fast fashion retailer. *Journal of Economic Geography*, 8(1), pp. 21–38.

Towers, N., Perry, P. & Chen, R. (2013). Corporate social responsibility in luxury manufacturer supply chains, A. Brun (ed.). *International Journal of Retail and Distribution Management*, 41(11/12), pp. 961–972.

Towers, N. & Song, Y. (2010). Future Challenges in Strategic Sourcing Garments from China. *Asia Pacific Business Review*, 16(4), pp. 527–544.

Wadhwa, S., Mishra, M., Chan, F. & Ducq, Y. (2010). Effects of information transparency and cooperation on supply chain performance: A simulation study. *International Journal of Production Research*, 48(1), pp. 145–166.

WBCSD (1999). *Report on Corporate Social Responsibility. Meeting Changing Expectations*. Geneva, Switzerland.

Weigel, R.H. (1977). Ideological and demographic correlates of proecology behaviour. *J Soc Psychol*, 103(1), pp. 39–47.

Wimer, P. (2001). *Increasing manufacturing responsiveness in the e-economy*. Available at: www.ascet.com/documents.asp?d_ID=291 [accessed 1 October 2017].

Wortmann, J.C. (1997). A typology of customer-driven manufacturing. *International Journal of Service Industry Management*, 6(2), pp. 59–73.

Zinn, W. & Bowersox, D.J. (1988). Planning physical distribution with the principle of postponement. *Journal of Business Logistics*, 9(2), pp. 117–136.

2

INTRODUCTION TO FASHION

2.1 The definition of fashion

Fashion clothing is a product with visible characteristics and it is able to build the self-image (Sha et al., 2007). Fashion has been defined as a widely behavioural phenomenon for both the tangible and intangible (Vieira, 2009). Kaiser has defined fashion as 'a form of collective behaviour that is socially approved at a given time but is expected to change' (Sha et al., 2007, p.454), while earlier, Evan (1989) pointed out that fashion releases both physical and mental dimensions of a person, and indirectly reflects the changes of people's health, life, etc.

2.1.1 Introduction to fashion characteristics

Fashion is a wild term that has four basic characteristics: short-lived, high volatility, low predictability, and with high impulse purchasing power (Christopher et al., 2004). The fashion market is highly competitive and needs to 'update' very frequently, which means fashion retailers have to renew their products and switch the fashion style frequently in order to follow up. The fashion market can be divided into several segments: luxury, high street and supermarket discounter (Bruce & Daly, 2006). High street fashion is the fashion style that can be easily reached by the public: not expensive, not scarce as luxury fashion, while fast fashion acted as a strategy by most of the high street fashion retailers recently (Abernathy et al., 1999).

2.1.2 The identification of consumer needs and fashion product

According to Park et al. (1986), there are three types of consumer needs: functional needs, symbolic needs and experiential needs. Functional needs are defined as needs which motivate the search for products and services that can resolve consumption-related issues (Park et al., 1986), such as solving an existing problem or preventing problems that may happen in future. Symbolic needs motivate consumers looking for the products which can 'fulfill internally generated needs' and for 'self-enhancement, role position, group membership or ego identification' (Park et al., 1986, p.136). Experiential needs are defined as the need for products that have 'sensory pleasure, variety and/or cognitive stimulation' (Park et al., 1986, p.136). Garvin (1987) indicated that fashion products can satisfy both symbolic needs and experiential needs.

2.1.3 Introduction to fashion industry

The fashion industry is at the forefront of emerging industries on a global level (Rocha et al., 2005). With consumers' need of a variety of products in the fashion market, the product introduction rate is increasing while the product cycle is shortening (Abernathy et al., 1999). Even in the mature European market, the fashion industry consists of continuous growth and development because of the short product cycle and the variety in products (Rocha et al., 2005). All these indicate that the fashion industry is developing with a rapid market and fashion enterprises should react faster in order to survive and keep in continuous development (Rocha et al., 2005).

2.1.4 UK and Chinese fashion market

With the nature of the UK's fashion clothing market, fashion retailers were in the market with high market concentration and format standardisation (Moore, 1996). With the interaction of high concentration and standardisation, there is lack of product differentiation on the UK high street (Birtwistle & Freathy, 1998).

The competition between UK fashion retailers is formed based on various retailers, such as Marks & Spencer; clothes in supermarkets such as George in Asda, and Tesco; discount retailers such as Primark and brand factory outlets (Birtwistle et al., 2003). Moreover, international fashion retailers such as Zara, Gap and H&M also increase the competition level in the UK fashion industry (Birtwistle et al., 2003), let alone the many emerging fashion enterprises such as Superdry and Monsoon. Thus, the UK fashion market is one of the most competitive due to its market structure and trading nature (Fernie & Corcoran, 2011). It is also hard for foreign fashion retailers to enter or penetrate the UK fashion market (Fernie & Corcoran, 2011). Fashion retailers occupied over one-third of all UK retailers in international markets (Groeschl & Doherty, 2000); many large fashion retailers such as Zara, Mango, Gap, and Marks & Spencer are in the process of internalising retailing due to the population of fashion retailers on the international stage (Fernie & Corcoran, 2011).

China is an emerging market with high purchasing power. Chinese economy growth is three times more compared to the USA over the last two decades (Hammond, 2000). With a population of approximately 1.3 billion in China, the

18 Introduction to fashion

consumer base is incredibly high (Census, 2011). With the open-door policy in 1978 in China, the country has achieved continued economic growth with average 8% gross domestic product (GDP) growth annually in recent years. With the sheer size of the market and the potential purchasing power, many global fashion retailers have started to enter the Chinese market (Gong, 2003). Some fast fashion retailers, such as Zara, Gap and H&M have already had a foot in the Chinese market for many years. It has brought more opportunities to the global retailers since China joined the World Trade Organization in 2003.

With the economic environment, the Chinese fashion market is attracting more foreign fashion retailers' attention (Delong et al., 2004). China provides many opportunities; however, it also leads to a high level of market competition (Delong et al., 2004). The global fashion retailers have to compete not only with the local fashion enterprises, but also the other international fashion retailers. Nevertheless, with the restrictive policies announced by the Chinese government – for example, the local enterprise protection policy – and the complex rules that apply to international fashion retailers, the developing process of foreign retailers is restricted on some levels (Delong et al., 2004).

2.2 Concepts of fashion

2.2.1 The evolution of fashion culture

'Fashion markets are synonymous with rapid change' (Christopher et al., 2004, p.1). One of the primary reasons for fashion change is from fashion retailers. With the fashion changes and new style updates, consumers are motivated to buy new clothes and other stuff continuously (Law et al., 2004). Getting through 'haute couture' and designer ready-to-wear, the fashion culture has switched to fast fashion recently (Tokatli, 2007).

The haute couture was represented by French designers and mostly 'French style': it was mostly dominated by the Parisian designers (Wenting & Frenken, 2007). Ready-to-wear fashion was the main segment in the fashion market during the post-Second World War period (Wenting & Frenken, 2007). If we say that 'haute couture' stands for the word 'customise', then ready-to-wear is standing as its opposite (Frank & Zeckhauser, 2007). Designers of haute couture considered ready-to-wear as too commercial and a threat to the high-standard haute couture (Frank & Zeckhauser, 2007). Different from haute couture and designer ready-to-wear, fast fashion retailers do not straight invest in design but search for the most attractive and fresh vogue trends that appear in the recent fashion shows (Agins, 1999; Reinach, 2005). Fast fashion retailers will transform the new fashion trends into products and send them to the market as soon as they can (Reinach, 2005). Without the design process, these fashion retailers can focus more on the expansion of store numbers, supply chain consolidation and development, strategy development and so forth.

The trend of fashion culture is moving from haute couture and designer ready-to wear to fast fashion. There is a powerful race among several giant fast fashion retailers about the expansion speed in a number of stores while with the best performance and most consolidated supply chains recently (Tokatli, 2007). The 'giant' fast fashion retailers such as the Spanish Zara, the Swedish H&M and American Gap were leading the way. Zara, which belongs to the Inditex Group, owned around 1,700 stores around the world at the end of 2010 (Inditex, 2010), while H&M owned around 2,200 stores (H&M, 2010) and Gap owned over 3,000 stores (Gap, 2010) until the end of 2010.

2.2.2 The concept of fast fashion

Fast fashion is the strategy that is frequently used by the high street fashion retailers. The main thought of fast fashion retailers is 'quick response' (Abernathy et al., 1999) – that is, the speed to transform the new fashions spotted in the fashion shows into products. Fast fashion retailers have to meet several requirements.

- Firstly, retailers should increase the number of stores around the globe rapidly with direct stores and outlets in secure countries and franchises in emerging/more risky ones, in order to get consumers across the world (Tokatli, 2007).
- Secondly, retailers have to connect consumer need with the design operation, production, procurement and distribution (Tokatli, 2007).
- Thirdly, short development cycles, limited quantity and quick response in order to let consumers have the latest fashion, also some exclusions are required (Tokatli, 2007).
- Fourthly, a fast and highly responsible supply chain is necessary in order to keep good performance and guarantee frequency in delivery (Reinach, 2005).
- Finally, as stock product performance has become the key measurement of success, a nice performance in stock is required (Tokatli, 2007).

The Spanish Zara, the Swedish H&M, the US-based Gap and British Topshop are some of the leading fast fashion retailers in the world. Nowadays the increasing numbers of stores alongside supply chains with maximum speed, synchronicity and responsiveness have become a significant way to measure the fast fashion retailers (Tokatli, 2007). According to the annual reports of each retailer, Zara, H&M, Gap and Topshop had approximately 1,700, 2,200, 3,000 and over 5,000 stores, including franchised stores, respectively. Meanwhile, the maximum speed, synchronicity and responsiveness of supply chains brings high dependability, flexibility and shorter lead times (Tokatli, 2007).

2.2.3 The age difference in the fashion market

The age factor is one big dimension involved in the fashion market segment (Auty & Elliott, 1998). Young adult consumers are important in the fashion market and

20 Introduction to fashion

this segment is the research target in many fashion studies (Workman & Kidd, 2000). Young adult consumers have potential power as they have the interest and optimism to try new stuff; the new fashions always begin from the young, side by side (Law et al., 2004). They are more involved in the fashion field than older people as they take more care about their appearance and self-image (O'Cass, 2004).

2.2.4 The youth in fashion segment

'Global marketers are drawn to teenagers' (Parker et al., 2004, p.176). There are several reasons to say that. First, the large size of the youth population makes the marketers focus on them. Second, the youth have significant purchasing power so that they are part of the trendsetters (Zollo, 1995). Based on the resources in 2002, US young adult spend was approximately $135 every month on fashion-related products and it occupied 34% of their free-allocated money (Chain Store Age, 2002). Third, compared to older consumers, they are more impressionable and they are in the process of forming brand loyalty. Moreover, as part of the young adult consumers are not economically independent, they are sponsored by family so that they may influence their family members' purchasing behaviour (Zollo, 1995).

2.3 Cultural dimension for fashion consumers

2.3.1 Culture influence

The purchase behaviour and decisions of purchase may be different between Western young consumers and Eastern young consumers (Law et al., 2004). This may because of the cultural difference between East and West. Hong Kong may be a special example because of its particular cultural background. Hong Kong used to be a colony of Great Britain for 100 years. The culture of Hong Kong combined and mixed both Eastern elements and Western elements (Law et al., 2004). In Hong Kong, young people desire and like to be fashionable and keep up to date (Tai & Tam, 1996). The cultural influence has an impact on consumer behaviour in purchasing fashion products (Law et al., 2004). In order to analyse the cultural difference between East and West, Hofstede's theories of the cultural difference between Eastern and Western will be discussed in this study. It may be helpful in finding how cultural difference influences the decision to purchase by young consumers in East and West.

2.3.2 Introduction to Hofstede's cultural dimension theories

'Culture' is the term that used to account for the differences between societies (Rubery & Grimshaw, 2003). The differences in culture can explain a lot of things, such as the decision making by consumers within different societies.

Hofstede is one of the greatest social psychologists who focuses on culture analysis in modern nations over the world (Hofstede, 2001). In Hofstede's words,

Introduction to fashion   21

culture is the 'collective programming of the mind that distinguishes one group or category of people from another' (Hofstede, 1993, p.5). Hofstede indicated that culture 'is always a collective phenomenon' which 'consist[s of] unwritten rules' and culture is learned when people are in societies, it is not innate (Hofstede et al., 1994, p.5).

Hofstede also indicated that national culture always has four different dimensions after researching people over 40 countries (Hofstede, 1983), which included: individualism/collectivism, power distance, uncertainty avoidance and masculinity/femininity.

2.3.3 Individualism and collectivism

Individualism and collectivism refer to the strength of the interrelationship between people within the society. In a more individualistic culture the connection between people is looser and people tend to look after themselves and fellow individuals such as their immediate family. While a more collectivist culture reflects a tight relationship between individuals. People are supposed to look after their ingroup and, conversely, the ingroup will help and protect them if they fall into trouble. Hofstede found that the rate of individualism is related to the countries' wealth. Highly developed countries such as Germany, the USA and Sweden showed a higher degree of individualism, while many developing countries such as Thailand, the Philippines and Iran showed a higher degree of collectivism (Hofstede, 1983).

2.3.4 Power distance

Power distance refers to the rate of inequality that exists and the acceptance level of people in the society. Hofstede indicates that people are unequal in society from birth, for both physical and intellectual capabilities. All societies are unequal, but to different degrees (Hofstede, 1983). In Hofstede's research, he found that there is a cosmopolitan relationship between rate of individualism and power distance, where collectivist countries are always combined with large power distance, such as the Philippines or India; poor countries exist with large power distance. However, individualist countries do not always have small power distance, such as France and Italy, which are countries with an individualist culture but relatively large power distance (Hofstede, 1983).

2.3.5 Uncertainty avoidance

The third dimension is uncertainty avoidance. Hofstede indicates that the future is unknown, and people have to live with uncertainties. Uncertainty avoidance refers to the degree of acceptance and tolerance of people when facing uncertainties. People in societies with weak uncertainty avoidance are relatively tolerant to the behaviour or effect which is different to their own and take risks relatively easier, as they do not feel threatened by the uncertainties. People with strong uncertainty avoidance are 'trying to beat the future'. As the future is always unpredictable, in

22 Introduction to fashion

this kind of society, people with strong uncertainty avoidance feel great nervousness and aggressiveness. They are trying to avoid the uncertainty and risk rather than accept it. Countries such as Japan, Germany and Greece have strong uncertainty avoidance, while countries such as Singapore, the UK and most of Northern Europe have weak uncertainty avoidance (Hofstede, 1983).

2.3.6 Masculinity and femininity

Masculinity and femininity describe the division of a society's role as rather masculine or feminine. It identifies the societies by 'sex role division'. A more masculine culture is focused more on career, performance and earnings, with less emphasis on caring for others and less focus on the quality of life. A more feminine culture focuses more on the quality of life, interpersonal relationships, the arts, caring and environment. In a masculine society, a public hero is successful, while in a feminine society, individual brilliance is more important. Countries such as Japan, Germany and the USA tend to be masculine societies, while countries such as France, Singapore and Denmark tend to be more feminine (Hofstede, 1983).

2.3.7 New dimension: long-term vs short-term orientation

The long-term and short-term orientation dimension was mentioned by Hofstede and Bond in 1988. It reflects the Eastern values and the concept of Confucius (Hofstede & Bond, 1988). Higher scores in the long-term orientation index refer to a more stable society and high respect for tradition; lower scores in the long-term orientation index refer to a more creative and novel society (Leo et al., 2005). According to Hofstede and Bond, China came relatively high on the long-term orientation index, while the UK came relatively low.

2.3.8 Criticism of Hofstede's cultural dimension theory

The cultural dimension theory is not perfect; some scholars have made some criticisms on Hofstede's theories. Ess and Sudweeks (2006) argued that Hofstede's theory had coverage issues, as it only researched on one firm, IBM, and one type of employee. Jacob (2005) argued that Hofstede didn't consider the multiculturalism issues; moreover, Rubery and Grimshaw (2003) critiqued the culture theories, indicating that cultural differences also occur within the countries: difference in gender, class, religion and region will also create different cultures.

The degree of individualism depends on a country's wealth, with higher developed countries always having higher rates of individualism, while lower wealth always indicates a collectivist country. Collectivist countries always have large power distance while individual countries do not always have small power distance. Countries with lower life pressure always have weak uncertainty avoidance as the uncertainty cannot threaten people; nevertheless, these countries are often feminine countries, such as those of Northern Europe, and Singapore, while countries with higher life pressure always have strong uncertainty avoidance and also a more masculine society, such as Japan and Greece.

Although there has been some criticism of the theory, Hofstede's cultural dimensions are helpful in analysing the purchase decisions of consumers. With cultural differences people make decisions differently. People in collectivist societies with large power distance may choose fashions with lower prices as they may not have the ability to afford the high-quality and expensive fashions; people from masculine societies may make decisions faster and may not care about the quality of the clothes and accessories as they care less about quality of life.

2.4 Consumers' decision-making process

The consumer decision process was first introduced by John Dewey in 1910. According to Dewey, there are five stages included in the consumer's decision-making process: problem recognition, information search, evaluation of the alternatives, choice making, and results (Bruner & Pomaza, 1988). The theory has been widely accepted and improved ever since. In 1978, Engel et al. established the consumer purchasing decision process based on Dewey's theory, which also included five stages: the problem awareness and need recognition, information search, evaluation of product options, purchase decision, and post-purchase evaluation (Engel et al., 1978).

2.4.1 Problem recognition

The consumer decision-making process begins at the problem recognition stage. Problem recognition acts as a 'cornerstone in the consumer decision process', and is based on two main parts: the desired state and the actual state (Bruner & Pomaza, 1988, p.61). The former indicates the need that would like to be achieved or something that is desired by a person; while the latter indicates the need that is actually achieved (Bruner & Pomaza, 1988). When there is a large difference between the two states with respect to a particular need or desired item, the problem recognition occurs (Bruner & Pomaza, 1988). For example, when a person is extremely thirsty, he desires water; there occurs a significant difference between the desired state and the actual state, and thus the problem recognition occurs.

Moreover, problem recognition can be either narrow or broad. For the former, there may only be one brand or one kind of product that can satisfy the consumer's need – for example, the consumer only wants the T-shirt from Superdry. The latter identifies a more generic problem recognition – for example, one could be hungry and simply have something to eat.

2.4.2 Information search

The second stage in the decision-making process is the information search. The information search helps a consumer to get the detailed information about the product in order to make a decision. According to Crotts, the information search

24 Introduction to fashion

can be divided into an internal information search and external information search (Crotts, 1999). The former indicates the search in a person's long-term memory, while the latter indicates information from an external source. According to Beatty and Smith, there are four types of external sources: 1 personal sources, such as advice from family or friends; 2 commercial sources, such as the advertisements, advice from a salesman and retailers; 3 public sources, such as advice from magazines, the internet, TV; 4 experimental sources, such as a visit or inspection of the stores before purchase (Beatty & Smith, 1987). In Beatty and Smith's point of view, an individual who doesn't have much product knowledge will tend to choose personal sources, as they may be threatened by and not trust the commercial and public sources; they are likely to gain the information from family members or friends (Beatty & Smith, 1987). Egoistic and self-concerned individuals are more likely to use public sources, while the individuals who care highly about the purchase are more likely to use experimental sources.

2.4.3 Alternative evaluation

The third stage in the consumer decision-making process is to evaluate the alternatives. The evaluation involves a comparison between price, quality, brand, effects, etc. (Gupta et al., 2004). With examination and comparison between the different options, consumers can figure out what they want.

During this stage, consumers may also evaluate the perceptive risk that may be involved. According to Slovic (1987), two components are involved in the perceptive risk: uncertainty and consequence. Uncertainty occurs when a consumer is not familiar with the product they bought, while negative consequence indicates the results after using the product (Slovic, 1987). For example, the perceptive risk would rise if a consumer is thinking of buying some spirits that he is not familiar with, as this consumer does not know the taste of the spirits (uncertainty) and does not know the responses of his friends after tasting the spirits (consequence) (Gupta et al., 2004). Technically, the consumer will consider all the elements such as price, quality, brand, risks, etc. before making a decision (Slovic, 1987).

2.4.4 Purchase decision

There exist difficulties even in the choice-making stage (Bettman et al., 1993). The difficulty of a purchase decision may increase with the rise in alternative quantity, or large uncertainty involved in the product (Bettman et al., 1993). Once the choice is made, the decision process is about to finish.

2.4.5 Post-purchase evaluation

The final stage in the consumer decision-making process is the post-purchase evaluation. Consumers often evaluate their decisions after purchase. In Gardial et al.'s words, 'consumers are typically motivated to evaluate products with particular use purposes and situations in mind' (Gardial et al., 1994, p.549). Product evaluation, such as comparison between brands and quality, is strongly related to pre-purchase evaluation (Park, 1980), while according to Ford, some product characteristics, such as level of comfort, taste, duration, can only be evaluated or easily judged by consumers after use (Ford et al., 1990). If the product is purchased online and is not a digital product or service, then the product still has to be delivered to the consumer's location (Gupta et al., 2004). Thus the delivery efficiency will become an important concern for both consumer and enterprise (Gupta et al., 2004). A post-purchase evaluation may consist of the cognitive process resulting in the judgement of the product, such as 'good/bad performed product'; and emotional response, such as 'I feel angry about the product' (Gardial et al., 1994). Post-purchase evaluation will influence the consumer's next purchasing choices; consumers may re-purchase the product or switch brand or product (Geva & Goldman, 1989).

References

Abernathy, Frederick H., Dunlop, John T. & Hammond, Janice H. (1999). *A Stitch in Time: Lean Retailing and the Transformation of Manufacturing – Lessons from the Apparel and Textile Industries*. New York and Oxford: Oxford University Press.

Agins, T. (1999). *The End of Fashion: How Marketing Changed the Clothing Industry Forever*. New York: Quill.

Auty, S. & Elliott, R. (1998). Fashion involvement, self-monitoring and the meaning of brands. *Journal of Product & Brand Management*, 7(2), pp. 109–123.

Beatty, S.E. & Smith, S.M. (1987). External search efforts: An investigation across several product categories. *Journal of Consumer Research*, 14, pp. 83–95.

Bettman, J.R., Johnson, E.J. & Payne, J.W. (1993). 'Consumer Decision Making', in T.S. Robertson & H.H. Kassarjian (eds), *Handbook in Consumer Behavior*. Englewood Cliffs, New Jersey: Prentice Hall, pp. 50–84.

Bettman, R.J., Payne, W.J. & Johnson, J.E. (1988). Adaptive Strategy Selection in Decision Making. *Journal of Experimental Psychology: Learning, Memory, and Cognition*, 14(3), pp. 534–552.

Birtwistle, G. & Freathy, P. (1998). More than just a name above the shop: A comparison of the branding strategies of two UK fashion retailers. *International Journal of Retail & Distribution Management*, 26(8), pp. 318–323.

Birtwistle, G., Siddiqui, N. & Fiorito, S. (2003). Quick response: Perceptions of UK fashion retailers. *International Journal of Retail & Distribution Management*, 31(2), pp. 118–128.

Bruce, M. & Daly, L. (2006). Buyer behaviour for fast fashion. *Journal of Fashion Marketing and Management*, 10(3), pp. 329–344.

Bruner, Gordon C. & Pomaza, Richard J. (1988). Problem Recognition: The Crucial First Stage of the Consumer Decision Process. *Journal of Consumer Marketing*, 5(1), pp. 53–63.

Census (2011). National bureau statistics of China. Available at: www.stats.gov.cn/english/newsandcomingevents/t20110428_402722237.htm [accessed 5 December 2016].

Chain Store Age (2002). Teens spending more, 78(5), pp. 35.

Christopher, M., Lowson, R. & Peck, H. (2004). Creating agile supply chains in the fashion industry. *International Journal of Retail & Distribution Management*, 32(8), pp. 367–376.

Crotts, J. (1999). 'Consumer Decision Making and Prepurchase Information Search, in Yoel Mansfield & Abraham Pizam (eds), *Consumer Behavior in Travel and Tourism*. Binghamton, NY: Haworth Press, pp. 149–168.

Delong, M., Bao, M.X., Wu, J.J., Chao, H. & Li, M. (2004). Perception of US branded apparel in Shanghai. *Journal of Fashion Marketing and Management*, 8(2), pp. 141–153.

Engel, J.F., Blackwell, R.D. & Kollat, D.T. (1978). *Consumer Behavior*. Hinsdale, IL: Dryden Press.

Ess, C. & Sudweeks, F. (2006). Culture and computer-mediated communication: Toward new understandings. *Journal of Computer-mediated Communication*, 11(1), pp. 179–191.

Evan, M. (1989). Consumer behaviour towards fashion. *European Journal of Marketing*, 23(7), pp. 7–16.

Fernie, J. & Corcoran, L. (2011). Responses to out-of-stocks and on-shelf availability in UK fashion retailing. *The International Review of Retail, Distribution and Consumer Research*, 21 (4), pp. 309–322.

Ford, G., Smith, B.D. & Swasy, L.J. (1990). Consumer Skepticism of Advertising Claims: Testing Hypotheses from Economics of Information. *Journal of Consumer Research*, 16(4), pp. 433–441.

Frank, R.G. & Zeckhauser, R.J. (2007). Custom-made versus ready-to-wear treatments: Behavioral propensities in physicians' choices. *Journal of Health Economics*, 26, pp. 1101–1127.

Gap (2010). *GAP 2010 Annual Report*. Available at: http://media.corporate-ir.net/media_files/IROL/11/111302/GPS_AR_10.pdf [accessed 31 October 2016].

Gardial, F.S., Clemons, S.D., Woodruff, B.R., Schumann, W.D. & Burns, J.M. (1994). Comparing consumers' recall of pre-purchase and post-purchase product evaluation experiences. *Journal of Consumer Research*, 20(4), pp. 548–560.

Garvin, D.A. (1987). Competing on the eight dimension of quality. *Harvard Business Review*, 65(6), pp. 101–108.

Geva, A. & Goldman, A. (1989). Duality in consumer post-purchase attitude. *Journal of Economic Psychology*, 12, pp. 141–164.

Gong, W. (2003). Chinese consumer behavior: A cultural framework and implications. *Journal of Academy of Business*, 3(1/2), pp. 373.

Groeschl, S. & Doherty, L. (2000). Conceptualizing culture. *Cross Cultural Management: An International Journal*, 7(4), pp. 12–17.

Gupta, A., Su, B. & Walter, Z. (2004). An Empirical Study of Consumer Switching from Traditional to Electronic Channel: A Purchase Decision Process Perspective. *International Journal of Electronic Commerce*, 8(3), pp. 131–161.

Hammond, A. (2000). *Which World? Global Destinies, Regional Choices*. Washington, DC: Island Press.

H&M (2010). *H&M Annual Report 2010*. Available at: www.eyemag.se/core/main.php?&SITEID=9b139&PROJECTNR=4170& [accessed 31 October 2016].

Hofstede, G. (1983). *The cultural relativity of organizational practice and theories*. Institute for Research on Intercultural Cooperation (IRIC), pp. 75–89.

Hofstede, G. (1993). Cultural constraints in management theories. *Academy of Management Executive*, 71(1), pp. 81–94.

Hofstede, G. (2001). *Culture's consequences: Comparing values behaviours, institutions and organisations across nations*. London: Sage Publications.

Hofstede, G. & Bond, M.H. (1988). The Confucius Connection: From Cultural Roots to Economic Growth. *Organizational Dynamics*, 16(4), pp. 4–21.

Hofstede, G., Hofstede, J.G. & Minkov, M. (1994). *Cultures and Organizations: Software of the Mind: Intercultural Cooperation and its Importance for Survival*. McGraw-Hill.

Inditex (2010). *Group Inditex Annual Report 2010*. Available at: www.inditex.es/en/sharehol ders_and_investors/investor_relations/annual_reports [accessed 1 November 2016].

Jacob, N. (2005). Cross-cultural investigations: Emerging concepts. *Journal of Organizational Change Management*, 18(5), pp. 514–528.

Law, K.M., Zhang, Z.M. & Leung, C.S. (2004). *Fashion change and fashion consumption: The chaotic perspective*. Institute of Textiles and Clothing, The Hong Kong Polytechnic University.

Leo, C., Bennett, R. & Härtel, C.E.J. (2005). Cross-cultural differences in consumer decision-making styles. *Cross Cultural Management: An International Journal*, 12(3), pp. 32–62.

Moore, C.M. (1996). La mode sans frontières? The internationalisation of fashion retailing. *Journal of Fashion Marketing and Management*, 1(4), pp. 345–356.

O'Cass, A. (2004). Fashion clothing consumption: Antecedents and consequences of fashion clothing involvement. *European Journal of Marketing*, 38(7), pp. 869–882.

Park, C.W. (1980). Effects of Prior Knowledge and Experience and Phase of the Choice Process on Consumer Decision Processes. *Journal of Consumer Research*, pp. 234–248.

Park, C.W., Jaworski, B.J. & MacInnis, D.J. (1986). Strategic brand concept-image management. *Journal of Marketing*, 50(4), pp. 135–145.

Parker, R.S., Hermans, M.C. & Schaefer, D.A. (2004). Fashion consciousness of Chinese, Japanese and American teenagers. *Journal of Fashion Marketing and Management*, 8(2), pp. 176–186.

Reinach, S.S. (2005). China and Italy: Fast fashion versus prêt a porter – towards a new culture of fashion. *Fashion Theory*, 9(1), pp. 43–56.

Rocha, V.M.A., Hammond, L. & Hawkins, D. (2005). Age, gender and national factors in fashion consumption. *Journal of Fashion Marketing and Management*, 9(4), pp. 380–390.

Rubery, J. & Grimshaw, D. (2003). *The Organisation of Employment: An International Perspective*. Palgrave Macmillan, pp. 26–50.

Sha, O., Aung, M., Londerville, J. & Ralston, E.C. (2007). Understanding gay consumers' clothing involvement and fashion consciousness. *International Journal of Consumer Studies*, 31(5), pp. 453–459.

Slovic, P. (1987). Perception of risk. *Science*, 236, pp. 280–285.

Tai, H.C. & Tam, L.M. (1996). A lifestyle analysis. *Journal of International Consumer Marketing*, 9(1), pp. 25–42.

Tokatli, N. (2007). Global sourcing: Insights from the global clothing industry – the case of Zara, a fast fashion retailer. *Journal of Economic Geography*, 8, pp. 21–38.

Vieira, V. (2009). An extended theoretical model of fashion clothing involvement. *Journal of Fashion Marketing and Management*, 13(2).

Wenting, R. & Frenken, K. (2007). *Firm Entry and Institutional Lock-in: An Organizational Ecology Analysis of the Global Fashion Design Industry*. Urban & Regional Research Centre Utrecht (URU), Utrecht University, Utrecht, The Netherlands.

Workman, E.J. & Kidd, K.L. (2000). Use of the need for uniqueness scale to characteristic fashion consumer groups. *Clothing and Textiles Research Journal*, 18, pp. 227–236.

Zollo, P. (1995). Talking to teens. *American Demographics*.

3

LEAN VS AGILE SUPPLY CHAIN

3.1 Introduction

This chapter discusses two possible solutions to the problem of volatile demand. This chapter suggests that the key to success is through the use of a more flexible and responsive supply chain that focuses on reducing time, such as lean and agile supply chain strategies. The agile and lean supply chain strategies will be examined in detail in order to compare and contrast their benefits and drawbacks as a solution to the problem of volatile demand. The chapter will conclude by describing the environment suitable for each solution. Finally, the chapter will offer insight into the 'leagile' supply chain strategy – a modern alterative to other traditional, commonly used supply chain strategies.

The fashion industry today is extremely fast paced and complex, and ever-changing in response to customer needs (Sterlacci & Arbuckle, 2006). Consumers are the driver of this unpredictable industry as demand is now more volatile than ever. The consumer market is challenging, with customers wanting new, updated products in store quicker than ever and also new collections being brought into store more frequently to increase their choices. The market as a whole is price sensitive (Evans & Harrigan, 2003); the demand from consumers determines whether the price of a product increases or decreases.

According to Christopher et al. (2004, p.367), 'conventional organizational structures and forecast driven supply chains are not adequate to meet the challenges of volatile and turbulent demand which typify fashion markets'. This shows that retailers now need to change their supply chains in order for them to react and respond to the changing consumer demand levels. A typically structured supply chain is no longer enough in order to be successful in the fashion market (Kurt Salmon, 2016). Consumer needs are changing at a much more frequent pace and there is increased expectation to deliver newness and refresh product ranges more frequently. This is supported by Mintel (2013), which states the keenest clothes shoppers aged under 35 are increasingly demanding not just in trend-led clothing but collections that are updated at least every six weeks, with a huge 48% agreeing with this. This has led to the number of seasons significantly increasing each year. According to Li (2009) product life cycles will continue to shorten, while demand will be increasingly difficult to forecast.

Having low costs is no longer enough to be successful in the fashion industry; one of the biggest success factors today is time. Hoek et al. (2001, p.126) stated 'the supply chain is now the dominant vehicle for competition'. This shows that having a quick supply chain that can react and respond to changing customer demand leads to a more successful business. Being the first to the market is crucial for success (Barnes & Lea-Greenwood, 2006). Customers will purchase from the first retailer to bring the products to market, so the later products go in store, the less chance they have of being successful. The supply chain needs the shortest lead time possible, whilst still producing good-quality, fashionable products.

3.2 Fashion supply chain – volatility

The fashion market is often referred to as volatile, characterised by 'short product lifecycles, low predictability and high impulse purchasing' (Christopher et al., 2004, p.367). It is highly important to consider the consumer when implementing a supply chain strategy as ultimately the success of the business will be determined by the marketplace and the consumer (Christopher & Towill, 2001).

A number of aspects related to consumer lifestyles have influenced the trend of volatile demand. One of these factors is the proliferation of popular culture, celebrities and magazines. Barnes and Lea-Greenwood (2010) suggest that these factors have increased consumers' desire for new trends and more importantly consumers want to buy into the new trends immediately. This presents a problem for retailers, as trends cannot be forecasted long in advance anymore. Retailers need to be able to react in the short amount of time in which trends catch on in order to exploit consumer demand.

Short product life cycles, low predictability and high impulse purchasing are all consequences of volatile demand in the fashion industry and present an obvious problem for supply chain management (Christopher et al., 2004), therefore suggesting that volatile demand has become a key competitive force in fashion retailing. In order to compete with the volatile demand of today there is a need for shorter lead times and quick response.

The supply chain can be used as a key tool for competitive advantage. The supply chain has been used to gain competitive advantage in the past (Christopher, 1998). It is now an essential tool for success. Barnes and Lea-Greenwood (2010) support the view that the crucial success factors for high street fashion today are both a fast turnaround and responsive design.

An improved supply chain can improve both market and financial performance (Qrunfleh & Tarafdar, 2013). The supply chain ultimately results in success that the

30 Lean vs agile supply chain

company would have not had otherwise (Christopher, 2001). Zara is benchmarked by many businesses and by academics as a successful fashion retailer due to its efficient supply chain (n.a., 2005), therefore highlighting the importance and benefits of an efficient supply chain in order to compete with volatile demand in the fashion industry today.

When trends appear, volatile demand means that competition is a lot more time sensitive (Gustafson et al., 2005). Therefore, it is clear that time and flexibility are key success factors in today's fashion industry, particularly in fast fashion (Barnes & Lea-Greenwood, 2006). Fast fashion involves using an improved and more efficient supply chain in order to respond to volatile consumer demand (Barnes & Lea-Greenwood, 2010). Sender (2013) states that fashion retailers need to become more flexible and have collections that can be produced at shorter notice in order to cope with unforeseen circumstances due to volatile consumer demand. Also, a supply chain's performance can be assessed by a number of factors, including flexibility and speed (Slack et al., 2010), therefore emphasising the importance of these factors in supply chain management.

Many academics discuss that time is not only a success factor but also a crucial factor in the fashion industry (Gustafson et al., 2005). In order to react to this competitive force retailers have adapted their supply chain to enable response to consumer demand and reduced lead times (Gustafson et al., 2005). This strategy can be defined as fast fashion, which has appeared in the apparel industry in recent years (Hansson, 2011). Fast fashion is commonly discussed as originating from a consumer lifestyle where the consumer has high awareness of fashion trends, little loyalty and high expectations of affordable clothing that is time relevant (Gabrielli, 2013). Volatile demand is the epitome of fast fashion, where timing is a priority and the aim is to deliver products in the shortest possible time (Bruce & Daley, 2006).

A responsive supply chain has been identified as a key solution to the problem of volatile demand in the fashion industry. This drives interest in the modern concept of agile supply chain strategies (Christopher, 2000) that focus on responsiveness (Christopher et al., 2004). The fact that the agile supply chain is a modern concept means literature regarding the benefits of agile supply chains can appear limited in comparison to the traditional lean supply chain; however, many academics are increasingly using Zara as a successful example of a company that reduces risk of volatile demand through increased responsiveness (Wu & Blackhurst, 2009).

Due to volatile demand, the supply chain has become increasingly crucial in order to compete in the fashion industry. Retailers are often seeking the latest and new innovation in the supply chain in order to have a time and responsiveness advantage. Many academics conclude or present the idea of the traditional lean approach and modern agile approach being combined (Mason-Jones et al., 2000). Christopher and Towill (2001) seem to be one of the pioneers of the so-called 'leagile' strategy. They discuss that a mix of agile and lean strategies could be more effective than the use of just one method, as it allows for high flexibility and low cost. This is highly relevant to the fashion industry where demand is volatile and price is no longer enough to compete (Hansson, 2011).

The literature review has identified volatile demand as a key problem, especially within the fashion industry. In summary, volatile demand is consumer demand that fluctuates regularly. It is characterised by low predictability, high impulse purchasing and short product life cycles. In order to compete against this competitive force retailers must adopt a supply chain strategy that offers short lead times and responsiveness as well as low cost. Retailers can take advantage of these benefits by utilising either the lean, agile or leagile strategy.

3.3 Agile supply chain

There has been some discussion of how fast fashion links with supply chain management, by responding with an agile strategy and quick response (Barnes & Lea-Greenwood, 2006). However, more commonly the agile supply chain is discussed in comparison to the lean supply chain. The two strategies have been compared due to the fact that they address the same application (Putnik & Putnik, 2012). Many other academics believe each strategy can be used in different contexts according to the variability and variety required (Christopher, 2000).

Agile and lean supply chain strategies are often discussed in the context of volatile consumer demand (Christopher et al., 2004; Qrunfleh & Tarafdar, 2013; Christopher, 2000). Although compared, they are distinguished as different strategies and used in various contexts. Distinctions are drawn between the two and many note that it is important that they should not be confused (Christopher & Towill, 2000; Christopher, 2000). The different strategies are sometimes described as opposites (Putnik & Putnik, 2012).

An agile supply chain can be used as a solution to the problem of volatile demand within the consumer market. Agility can be seen as a solution due to the level of 'customer responsiveness' (Christopher et al., 2001) that can be achieved and the ability to anticipate 'uncertainties' (Jackson & Johansson, 2003). An agile supply chain means one that allows for flexibility in manufacture and quick response to regular fluctuations. It allows products to be created with a high variability due to the quick change in manufacture. This makes agility important in the manufacture of goods with a short product life cycle (Childerhouse & Towill, 2000). This is essential for fast fashion products which can become obsolete with the introduction of the next season's trends. Features of an agile supply chain mean that products created can be of a low volume as small, specialised batches based on demand.

Agility can be obtained through the method of postponement. It is the method of creating a base product and then leaving the finalisation and specialisation to be done last so that it is in response to trends/demands of the season (Chaudhry & Hodge 2012). It will rely on data that can give exact information about the demand of the product. With the use of specific data it means that there is less likely to be the creation of an obsolete product, with risky fashion predictions many months in advance. The first phase of production (e.g. the fabric) is forecast with the second phase (e.g. dye colour) based on data that have been specifically gathered (Yang & Burns, 2003). Types of postponement include purchasing

32 Lean vs agile supply chain

postponement (e.g. raw materials) and manufacture postponement (Chaudhry & Hodge 2012). Lead times can be cut through the use of manufacture postponement, which allows for a higher certainty of creating the correct product. This solves the issue of volatility as low predictability can be accounted for and manufacture can be done in conjunction with the demand of the market.

Many academics including Christopher (2000), Gunasekaran et al. (2008) and Yusuf et al. (2004) all believe that agility is essential to enhance the responsiveness of the supply chain, allowing quicker response to changing consumer needs by aiming to be flexible. Qrunfleh and Tarafdar (2013) state that the greater the extent of agility in the supply chain, the greater its responsiveness to volatile demand. This highlights that an agile supply chain is a key solution to solving the problem of volatile demand.

Although many academics support a positive link between agile supply chains and responsiveness, Qrunfleh and Tarafdar (2013) argue that an agile supply chain alone does not directly create responsiveness. The postponement strategy that an agile supply chain incorporates increases flexibility and therefore enhances the relationship between the agile supply chain strategy and supply chain responsiveness. The principle of postponement is to carry inventory in a generic form (Christopher, 2000). A supply chain with the ability to hold materials undifferentiated until consumer demand is known will be able to respond quicker to these changes in consumer demand (Van Hoek, 1999; Lee, 2004).

Although agility can appear the ideal solution to the problem of volatile demand, it must be considered that implementing the measures necessary to increase agility can be challenging and complex. It may be difficult for a company to react quickly to changes in demand unless they are willing to significantly increase logistical investment (Prater et al., 2001).

3.3.1 Advantages and disadvantages of agile

To be successful in a changing environment, firms must be able to respond quickly to volatile demand. An advantage of an agile supply chain is quick response (see Table 3.1), which helps the company to meet consumer needs. Gould (1997) describes agile supply as the ability to succeed in an environment of rapid and unpredictable change. According to Christopher (2000), this is now essential for a successful fashion company as responsiveness increases competitive advantage (Goldman et al., 1995).

A second advantage to an agile supply chain that solves the problem of volatile demand is the ability to customise products (see Table 3.1). Instead of relying on predictions and forecasting, agility employs a 'wait-and-see' approach to demand, only committing to products when demand is identified (Goldsby et al., 2006). Zara's fabrics are produced in Portugal and Spain and are ordered uncoloured, giving them flexibility to change the colour depending on the trends. The ability to customise products locally means that a higher level of variety may be offered at lower total cost enabling mass customisation (Christopher, 2000).

Lean vs agile supply chain **33**

TABLE 3.1 Advantages and disadvantages of an agile supply chain

Advantages	Disadvantages
Quick response to changing consumer demand (Gould, 1997)	High cost of implementation if investment is needed (Prater et al., 2001)
Customisation to meet volatile consumer needs (Goldsby et al., 2006)	Hiring a multi-skilled workforce is expensive (Huang et al., 2002)
Flexibility to enable quick product changeovers (Christopher, 2000)	Wasted capacity by holding a wide variety of raw materials that can't be sold (Goldsby et al., 2006)
Lower inventory of finished products reduces risk of obsolescence (Goldsby et al., 2006)	Risk of compromising on speed, cost and quality (Gunasekaran et al., 2008)

Flexibility is a major advantage to an agile supply chain (see Table 3.1). According to Christopher (2000), this can be achieved through the postponement strategy, meaning the company is more flexible to use the same components to manufacture a variety of end products. Agile supply chains also have the ability to produce in large or small batches, allowing flexible product changeovers when demand changes. Furthermore, agile supply chains employ a flexible, multi-skilled workforce who can adapt to produce what the consumer demands (Goldsby et al., 2006). Flexibility and responsiveness is also achieved as supply should be located nearby, and information sharing among workers must be open and frequent (Christopher & Towill, 2001).

Table 3.1 shows that a further advantage of an agile supply chain is that a company can reduce costs through low inventory. In the fashion retail industry, products have short life cycles and erratic demand, where the risk of obsolescence is high (Goldsby et al., 2006). An agile company may hold materials that can be dyed and finished at a later date when there is real demand, then immediately sold at full price rather than holding finished inventory which is no longer demanded and forced to be marked down. Zara aims to reduce excess inventory in the supply chain and risk associated with forecasting as product specifications are not finalised until closer to delivery (Birtwistle et al., 2003), therefore only 15% of items are sold at a marked-down price, increasing profit. On the other hand, low inventory can increase a company's risk of running out of product (Lee, 2002).

On the other hand agile supply chains have potential drawbacks (see Table 3.1), especially relating to the cost of implementation. For example, it may be difficult for a global operating company that ships products by sea to serve niche markets with customised goods and promptly react to changes in demand (Prater et al., 2001). Therefore, unless the company is prepared to significantly increase logistics costs, responsiveness to volatile demand will not be achieved.

Multi-skilled workers are needed to enable production of different types of merchandise that consumers demand; however, training and hiring skilled workers (Huang et al., 2002) is expensive, and multi-skilled workers demand high wages.

34 Lean vs agile supply chain

A major issue with an agile supply chain is the high capitalisation often required for flexibility in the production and assembly areas to enable production of a wide variety of goods. The agile model also only takes the product from the raw material state to final assembly upon demand. As a result, raw material inventory will sit for a longer period of time, on average (Goldsby et al., 2006). This could be seen as a waste of money and resources.

An agile supply chain may also have negative effects if response to consumer pressures compromises on speed, cost and quality. Therefore agility should not only focus on responsiveness and flexibility to volatile demand, but also on cost and the quality of the product. (Gunasekaran et al., 2008).

3.4 Lean supply chain

Lean is a traditional business strategy, which originated with Toyota. It was later popularised by Womack et al. (1990) in their book *The Machine that Changed the World*, by applying the principles of lean production for the car industry. However, today, this concept has been widely applied throughout many industry sectors, such as the fashion industry, where it can be identified as a key solution to the problem of volatile demand.

Toyota has identified seven types of waste, which form the core of the lean philosophy: overproduction, waiting time, transport, process, inventory, motion and defectives. According to Slack et al. (2010, p.435), these seven types of waste contribute to four barriers to achieving lean synchronisation: waste from irregular flow, waste from inexact supply, waste from inflexible response, and waste from variability.

Hirakawa, Hoshino and Katayama (2007, p.56) express the need to 'develop integrated manufacturing systems which can respond flexibly to market demands'. It can be argued that the implementation of lean is an effective solution as it allows value derived from the consumer market to be 'translated back along the processes in the supply chain' (Lamming, 1996, p.183). Through streamlining production, focus is placed on the supply chain collectively with a specific emphasis on identifying and eliminating non-value-adding activities unbeneficial to the consumer. This allows for a more transparent view of the supply chain, facilitating minimisation of inventory, reducing overheads and lead times. Benefits are recognised by both consumer and retailer, as analysed by Goldsby, Griffis and Roath (2006).

One aspect of lean management is the application of just-in-time (JIT) manufacturing, which according to Schneider and Leatherman (1992, p.78) as cited by Wong and Johansen (2005) 'redefines the way we look at business practices'. The streamlined pull system of production focuses on market demand being the factor influencing manufacturing. JIT emphasises the consumer being central to business activities, which is essential in competitive markets such as retailing, where the volatile turbulent demand jeopardises businesses' chance of competitiveness, profitability and, most importantly, survival.

Lean vs agile supply chain **35**

The fact that 'lean typically relies on a much shorter forecast horizon' (Goldsby et al., 2006, p.60), provides businesses with more up-to-date market information, allowing increased flexibility as predictions are more accurate, therefore a business is able to react more efficiently to these turbulent fluctuations within the market. JIT facilitates further inventory and raw materials minimisation but does rely on successful implementation and 'coordination with supply chain to avoid delays in the production schedule' (Kootanaee et al., 2013, p.8).

Effective communication between JIT manufacturers and retailers is essential, ensuring capacity in terms of staff, raw materials and machinery is present when demanded, achieving flexible production. Effective implementation and coordination of JIT in the long term facilitates the potential for continued improvement of the supply chain, thus the ability to create a point of differentiation. Continued small improvements over time, known as 'kaizen', are a key element of the JIT philosophy, as expressed by Kootanaee, Babu and Talari (2013). This is shown through Zara's business model, as they are now benchmarked for their effective supply chain and ability to differentiate themselves in the market as a result, therefore achieving a strong market leader position.

3.4.1 Advantages and disadvantages of lean

There are numerous advantages and disadvantages for a lean supply chain (see Table 3.2). In terms of advantages, customer responsiveness is a great benefit for the lean strategy which, by having the finished product sitting in inventory for a shorter period of time, enables a more responsive method to short-term consumer demand – providing the customer with the right product as fast as possible.

Multiple academics, including Sezen (2009), claim that this lean business strategy is a way of improving quality in a more efficient manner by lowering the supply chain cost and achieving this with less effort. Although Greenberg (2002) argues that adhering to this concept can be expensive in times of emergency as the company will not have enough buffer inventories to react and keep the supply chain moving. The lean business strategy is described by many academics, such as Shah and Ward (2007), as a method of elimination of waste within and beyond the organisation's product value chain, which could lower the supply chain cost created by the volatile demand. According to Lu (2011, p.57), 'this

TABLE 3.2 Advantages and disadvantages of a lean supply chain

Advantages	Disadvantages
Customer responsiveness (Broyles, 2005)	Interdependence (Broyles, 2005)
Efficient production operations (Broyles, 2005)	Supply shocks (Greenberg, 2002)
Cost effectiveness (Sezen, 2009)	Insulation of the stages (Slack et al., 2010)

36 Lean vs agile supply chain

elimination of waste will have a direct and visible consequence' of reducing costs in the supply chain.

There are numerous advantages and disadvantages to a lean supply chain. In terms of advantages, customer responsiveness is a great benefit for the lean strategy which, by having the finished product sitting in inventory for a shorter period of time, enables a more responsive method to short-term consumer demand – providing the customer with the right product as fast as possible (Broyles, 2005).

A lean strategy equally provides more efficient production operations in terms of the reduction of set-up time and the simplification of inventory flow (Broyles, 2005). Fewer goods are kept in warehouses and, as a result, the flow of goods from warehouse to shelves improves. This is due to a reduction in the number and size of these warehouses and, therefore, reduced inventory volumes.

Large warehouses full of all different types of goods are time consuming to manage and involve keeping many inventories. It also costs a lot to hold a wide variety of stock – for the 'lean' business strategy this is not the case. However, making this business model work requires good forecasting and planning. The company has to fully understand its market in order to respond to the varying trends of the customer's needs. The lean business must be able to predict relatively accurately what they will sell in the coming weeks, and then be able to plan the manufacturing/distribution schedule to meet that forecast.

According to Broyles (2005), by having more efficient production operations, companies are not only more responsive to their customers, but they also have less capital tied up in raw materials and finished goods.

Focusing on training improves quality, another positive aspect of this type of supply chain strategy. By using money saved from reduced capital and warehousing costs the lean supply chain can provide a better-trained and more flexible workforce resulting in lower defect rates, thus giving a more streamlined production with less waste. Employees with multiple skills can also be used more efficiently; for example, staff can be moved to where they are most needed at any given time. Most importantly, improved quality results in greater consumer satisfaction.

Cost effectiveness is certainly an allure for using a lean approach. With the streamlined production and obvious cost advantage of holding less stock it becomes an attractive business model (Sezen, 2009).

However, it's important to consider the disadvantages. One drawback of this strategy is supply shocks: will the supplier be able to cope with the demand? There is a risk that a single supplier won't have the capacity to fulfil the order. Or, if there is a need for extra stock, staff may need to work overtime – would the supplier pass this cost to the JIT business? If so, the cost base of the garments would increase – thus having an impact on profit. 'In just-in-time, everything is very interdependent. Everyone relies on everyone else' (Greenberg, 2002, p.4). Another downside of this interdependence is that there is a high risk of the supplier having too much power in that they know they are the only supplier and thereby take advantage of this. For example, if demand shoots up unexpectedly, the supplier could choose to increase their prices because the JIT enterprise would have no immediate inventory to buffer the sudden, unplanned increase in demand. However, this can be avoided by building up a good relationship with the supplier.

Some other issues with depending on a particular supplier are, for example, unforeseen production interruptions (Broyles, 2005), market demand fluctuations, stock outs, and lack of communication throughout the supply chain. The latter, being termed the 'insulation of the stages' (Slack et al., 2010, p.432), is where a problem occurs at one stage along the business model but this may not be immediately apparent elsewhere in the system. The larger the stock, the more products you have as a buffer before it starts affecting the front line – i.e. the consumer. According to Greenberg (2002), the JIT concept can lead to increased costs in times of emergency.

These disadvantages are all linked to reduced inventory. This is probably the biggest risk area for the lean business model. If the company's buyers fail to adjust quickly to increased demand or if the suppliers have distribution problems, the business risks upsetting the consumer with stock outs. If buyers over-compensate and buy extra inventory to avoid stock outs, the company could experience higher inventory costs and the potential for waste – something it was trying to avoid in the first place by using the lean business model.

3.5 Similarities and differences

Lean is often referred to as the more traditional of the two strategies, as it has been popular for several years longer. Lean is also described as the antecedent to agility and agility is described as a derivative of the lean strategy (Putnik & Putnik, 2012; Robertson & Jones, 1999). Lean systems have been discussed for decades, with numerous chapters available, whilst, Christopher et al. (2004) state that there is 'a growing interest' in the agile supply chain. Lean and agile methods are often compared as they are supply chains that are specific in aiming to meet the needs of the consumer in the current volatile market (Table 3.3).

A similarity between the two supply chains is the reduced lead times that they both offer in comparison to a traditional supply chain. This solves the volatile consumer demand as products can go on sale as quickly as possible to meet their needs. Lead times are reduced in a lean supply chain as all non-value-adding activities are eliminated and 'by definition excess time is waste'

TABLE 3.3 Similarities and differences of lean and agile supply chains

Similarities	Differences
Reduced lead times (Mason-Jones et al., 2000; Yang & Burns, 2003)	Flexibility vs streamlined production (Castro et al., 2012; Lamming, 1996)
Reactive manufacturing (Chaudhry & Hodge, 2012; Bruce et al., 2004)	Lean is algorithmic; agile relies on shared information (Baramichai et al., 2007)
Aim to meet consumer demands at lowest cost (Bruce et al., 2004)	Resource capabilities (Mason-Jones et al., 2000)

38 Lean vs agile supply chain

(Mason-Jones et al., 2000, p.55). The JIT method means that stock is not waiting around in inventory, which would add to the lead time of the product. In an agile supply chain the flexibility in manufacture aims to cut the lead times as when the demand is known, postponement can go straight into production of the finishing elements of manufacture (Yang & Burns, 2003). Zara is an example of a fast fashion retailer that cuts down its lead times using manufacturing postponement (Chaudhry & Hodge, 2012).

Another similarity between the two types of supply chain is that they are reactive manufacturers. They both need information fed back into the system in order for the correct type or amount of stock to be made. This allows for the retailer to work off the information within the volatile demand in order to produce the correct amount or type of product. An agile supply chain uses information from a specific 'demand pattern' or from a consumer's direct request. Chaudhry and Hodge (2012) have named this point the 'order penetrating point' within the supply chain. This shows that the catalyst of the information is needed before the sequences from postponement can occur. This has the similarity with a lean supply chain as to avoid any waste and unnecessarily made products, production will only begin once information is passed through the supply chain from either electronic data interchange (EDI) or the use of barcodes (Bruce et al., 2004).

Lean and agile supply chains both tend to the volatile market but at the same time are aiming to keep profit levels up through the minimisation of waste product, therefore keeping the cost of the product lower. The waste product can be unsold items that are left in inventory which either can become obsolete due to the replacement of the trend or the input of the competition (Chaudhry & Hodge, 2012). A lean supply chain minimises the amount of waste through only creating the amount of stock that is needed. This is done through JIT systems and the use of EDI and barcodes (Bruce et al., 2004). An agile supply chain also creates a lower amount of unsold inventory as it isn't relying on predictions in anticipation of demand (Bruce et al., 2004). The product specifications being tailored to the stock needed means the accurate type of product is created.

The differences between lean and agile are key in the decisions businesses make regarding which strategy to choose. Both lean and agile integrate the consumer within the supply chain, which is essential for a company in developing competitiveness in a turbulent market (White & Pearson, 2001).

An agile supply chain focuses directly on the product and its flexibility, allowing quick product changeovers and the ability to utilise a 'make-to-order approach' fulfilling specialised orders directly from consumers. Upon comparison to lean differentiation the primary focus of lean is on the process of streamlining the supply chain, reducing non-value-adding activities and inventory, thus decreasing the time to market for consumers. This comparison is also expressed by Castro, Putnik and Shah (2012), who identify the main difference between the two being the degree of product volume: lean was created for the masses (high volume), whereas agile for individuals (low volumes, due to customisation). Lamming (1996, p.184) observes that 'a truly lean system would lack the basic flexibility necessary for it to function in a real situation. This flexibility might take the form of time to think'. Agile supply chains do have greater flexibility through greater ability to cope with destination changes, production dates, schedules and even a change in order quantities. However, it is key to note that 'different companies experience different sets of changes and require different degrees of agility' (Baramichai et al., 2007, p.336), and which one a company chooses depends on individual business aims, type of product sold as well as placing consideration on the market it operates in.

Lean requires that the supply chain use the least amount of resources to efficiently complete manufacturing jobs, which is beneficial to businesses through the ability to 'obtain the highest levels of usage out of limited resources available' (Kootanaee et al., 2013, p.9). This decreases business costs, whilst ensuring the end consumer still receives a quality product when demand for it is required. A truly lean system will ensure value is transferred to the end consumer, in the most cost-effective but efficient way possible, allowing the businesses better chance at survival (Lamming, 1996). In comparison, agile supply chains require more machinery choice and capacity to be left spare to be able to fulfil specialised orders directly to consumers, in the most efficient way possible. Agile also requires multi-skilled employees to be able to complete a variety of tasks as dictated by the demand situation. Overall, product variety is high for agile supply chains and low for lean supply chains, which also limits the number of industries that lean is suited to (Mason-Jones et al., 2000).

3.6 Summary

Solutions to the problem of volatile consumer demand have been identified, all of which offer speed, low cost and responsiveness, which are proven success factors in the fashion industry. In order to solve the problem of volatile consumer demand, retailers need to adopt a supply chain strategy that aims to reduce lead times and reacts to consumer demands. After critically analysing both lean and agile supply chain strategies it is clear that each strategy can provide a certain competitive advantage in order to solve the problem of volatile consumer demand. Primarily, the lean strategy provides efficiency, whereas the agile strategy provides responsiveness. However, in today's competitive market it would be beneficial to have both advantages.

Choosing between strategies will depend on a number of factors, including the nature of the market which the retailer operates in. Fast fashion requires a highly responsive supply chain, therefore an agile supply chain would be the most suitable solution, whereas a retailer producing commodity products would be more suited to a lean supply chain, due to its continuous production line. The operational and strategic objectives of the business would have to be taken into account when deciding upon the best supply chain strategy. It depends upon the long-term goals of the business, and their day-to-day objectives, as to whether they choose a lean or agile supply chain.

Leagile (Naylor et al., 1997) is a supply chain strategy that uses aspects of both lean and agile strategies in order to reduce the time to market and respond to consumer demands. Zara is benchmarked by many businesses due to its use of the leagile strategy. Their staple goods with certain demand and high volume take on a lean approach, whilst their fast fashion goods with unpredictable demand and low volume are produced within an agile supply chain. It is important to note that although many companies aim to be like Zara and leagile may seem like the best option for all companies, proper analysis and thought needs to be carried out to decide on its suitability for a particular company as it requires a high amount of resources and finance. In an ideal world the Zara leagile supply chain would be replicated by everyone but in reality it is very difficult to implement, therefore an agile strategy may be more appropriate.

References

Baramichai, M., Zimmers, E. & Marangos, C. (2007). Agile supply chain transformation matrix: An integrated tool for creating an agile enterprise. *Supply Chain Management: An International Journal*, 12(5), pp. 334–348.

Barnes, L. & Lea-Greenwood, G. (2006a). Fast fashion in the retail store environment. *International Journal of Retail & Distribution Management*, 38(10), pp. 760–772.

Barnes, L. & Lea-Greenwood, G. (2006b). Fast fashioning the supply chain: Shaping the research agenda. *Journal of Fashion Marketing and Management*, 10(3), pp. 259–271.

Barnes, L. & Lea-Greenwood, G. (2010). Fast fashion in the retail store environment. *International Journal of Retail & Distribution Management*, 38(10), pp. 760–772.

Birtwistle, G., Siddiqui, N. & Fiorito, S. (2003). Quick response: Perceptions of UK fashion retailers. *International Journal of Retail & Distribution Management*, 31(2), pp. 118–128.

Blome, C., Schoenherr, T. & Rexhausen, D. (2013). Antecedents and enablers of supply chain agility and its effect on performance: A dynamic capabilities perspective. *International Journal of Production Research*, 51(4), pp. 1295–1318.

Broyles, L.C. (2005). *Resilience: Its Relationship to Forgiveness in Older Adults*. PhD diss., University of Tennessee. Available at: http://trace.tennessee.edu/utk_graddiss/1868 [accessed January 2018].

Bruce, M. & Daly, L. (2006). Buyer behaviour for fast fashion. *Journal of Fashion Marketing and Management*, 10(3), pp. 329–344.

Bruce, M., Daly, M. & Towers, N. (2004). Lean or agile: A solution for supply chain management in the textiles and clothing industry? *International Journal of Operations & Production Management*, 24(2), pp. 151–170.

Castro, H., Putnik, G. & Shah, V. (2012). A review of agile and lean manufacturing as issues in selected international and national research and development programs and roadmaps. *Learning Organization*, 19(3), pp. 267–289.

Chaudhry, H. & Hodge, H. (2012). Postponement and supply chain structure: Cases from the textile and apparel industry. *Journal of Fashion Marketing and Management*, 16(1), pp. 64–80.

Childerhouse, P. & Towill, D. (2000). Engineering supply chains to match customer requirements. *Logistics Information Management*, 13(6), pp. 337–346.

Christopher, M. (1998). Logistics and Competitive Strategy. *Logistics Information Management*, 1(4), pp. 204–206.

Christopher, M. (2000). The Agile Supply Chain: Competing in Volatile Markets. *Industrial Marketing Management*, 29(1), pp. 37–44.

Christopher, M., Lowson, R. & Peck, H. (2004). Creating agile supply chains in the fashion industry. *International Journal of Retail & Distribution Management*, 32(8), pp. 367–376.

Christopher, M. & Towill, D. (2000). Supply chain migration from lean and functional to agile and customised. *Supply Chain Management: An International Journal*, 5(4), pp. 206–213.

Christopher, M. & Towill, D. (2001). An integrated model for the design of agile supply chains. *International Journal of Physical Distribution & Logistics Management*, 31(4), pp. 235–246.

Evans, C. & Harrigan, J. (2003). *Distance, time, and specialization*. International Finance Discussion Papers, 766. Board of Governors of the Federal Reserve System (US).

Gabrielli, V.B. (2013). Consumption practices of fast fashion products: A consumer-based approach. *Journal of Fashion Marketing and Management: An International Journal*, pp. 206–224.

Gabrielli, V., Baghi, I. & Codeluppi, V. (2000). Consumption practices of fast fashion products: A consumer-based approach. *Journal of Fashion Marketing and Management*, 17(2), pp. 206–224.

Goldman, S., Nage, R. & Preiss, K. (1995). *Agile Competitors and Virtual Organizations: Strategies for Enriching the Customer*. New York: Van Nostrand Reinhold Company.

Goldsby, T., Griffis, S. & Roath, A. (2006). Modeling Lean, Agile and Leagile Supply Chain Strategies. *Journal of Business and Logistics*, 27(1), pp. 60–61.

Gould, P. (1997). What is agility? *Manufacturing Engineer*, 76(1), pp. 28–31.

Greenberg, D. (2002). *Just-In-Time Inventory System Proves Vulnerable to Labor Strike*. Los Angeles: Los Angeles Business Journal.

Gunasekaran, A., Laib, K. & Cheng, T.C. Edwin (2008). Responsive supply chain: A competitive strategy in a networked economy. *Omega*, 36(4), pp. 549–564.

Gustafson, A., Von Schmiesing-Korff, A. & Sze Lit, N. (2005). *A Time Efficient Supply Chain Model for an Apparel Company*. Sweden: Kristianstad Business School.

Hansson, M. (2011). *What impact has a fast fashion strategy on fashion companies' supply chain management?* Sweden: Halmstad University.

Hirakawa, Y., Hoshino, K. & Katayama, H. (2007). A Hybrid Push/Pull Production Control System for Multistage Manufacturing Processes. *International Journal of Operations & Production Management*, 12(4), pp. 69–81.

Hoek, R., Harrison, A. & Christopher, M. (2001). Measuring agile capabilities in the supply chain. *International Journal of Operations & Production Management*, 21(1), pp. 126–148.

Huang, S., Uppal, M. & Shi, J. (2002). A product driven approach to manufacturing supply chain selection. *Supply Chain Management: An International Journal*, 7(4), pp. 189–199.

Jackson, M.C. & Johansson, C. (2003). An agility analysis from a production system perspective. *Integrated Manufacturing System*, 14(6), pp. 482–488.

Kootanaee, A., Babu, K. & Talari, H. (2013). Just-in-Time Manufacturing System: From Introduction to Implement. *International Journal of Economics*, 1(2), pp. 7–25.

Kurt Salmon (2016). How to succeed in a disintermediated world, April. Available at: www. kurtsalmon.com/en-us/Retail/vertical-insight/1550/How-to-Succeed-in-a-Disintermediated-World [accessed 15 September 2017].

Lamming, R. (1996). Squaring lean supply with supply chain. *International Journal of Operations & Production Management*, 16(1), pp. 183–196.

Lee, H. (2002). Aligning Supply Chain Strategies with Product Uncertainties. *California Management Review*, 44(3), pp. 105–119.

Lee, H. (2004). The triple-A supply chain. *Harvard Business Review*, 82(10), pp. 102–112.

Li, Cai-fen (2009). Agile Supply Chain. *Management Science and Engineering*, 3(2).

Li, S., Ragu-Nathan, B., Ragu-Nathan, T. & Rao, S. (2006). The impact of supply chain management practices on competitive advantage and organizational performance. *Omega*, 34(2), pp. 107–124.

Lu, D. (2011). *Fundamentals of Supply Chain Management*. London: Ventus Publishing. p. 57.

Mason-Jones, R., Naylor, B. & Towill, D. (2000). Engineering the leagile supply chain. *International Journal of Agile Management Systems*, 2(1), pp. 54–61.

Mintel (2013). *Clothing Retail Executive Summary*. Available: http://academic.mintel.com/display/638286/ [accessed 29 April 2014].

Mitra, A. & Bhardwaj, S. (2010). Alignment of supply chain strategy with business strategy. *IUP Journal of Supply Chain Management*, 7(4), pp. 49–65.

n.a. (2005). How Zara fashions its supply chain: Home is where the heart is. *Strategic Direction*, 21(10), pp. 28–31.

Narasimhan, R., Kim, S. and Tan, K. (2008). An empirical investigation of supply chain strategy typologies and relationships to performance. *International Journal of Production Research*, 46(18), pp. 1–29.

Naylor, J.B., Naim, M.M. & Berry, D. (1997). *Leagility: Integrating the lean and agile manufacturing paradigm in the total supply chain*. MASTS working chapter No. 47. (Re-published in *International Journal of Production Economics* (1999), 62, pp. 107–118.)

Prater, E., Biehl, M. & Smith, M. (2001). International Supply Chain Agility: Tradeoffs Between Flexibility and Uncertainty. *International Journal of Operations and Production Management* 21(5), pp. 823–839.

Putnik, G. & Putnik, Z. (2012). Lean vs agile in the context of complexity management in organizations. *Learning Organization*, 19(3), pp. 248–266.

Qi, Y., Zhao, X. & Sheu, C. (2011). The impact of competitive strategy and supply chain strategy on business performance: The role of environmental uncertainty. *Decision Sciences*, 42(2), pp. 371–389.

Qrunfleh, S. & Tarafdar, M. (2013). Lean and agile supply chain strategies and supply chain responsiveness: The role of strategic supplier partnership and postponement. *Supply Chain Management: An International Journal*, 18(6), pp. 571–582.

Robertson, M. & Jones, C. (1999). Application of lean production and agile manufacturing concepts in a telecommunications environment. *International Journal of Agile Management Systems*, 1(1), pp. 14–17.

Schneider, J.D. & Leatherman, M.A. (1992). Integrated just-in-time: A total business approach. *Production and Inventory Management Journal*, 33(1), pp. 78–82.

Sender, T. (2013). *Review of 2013 Consumer Trends in the Clothing Market*. Available: http://academic.mintel.com/display/690570/?highlight [accessed 26 March 2014].

Sezen, B. & Erdogan, S. (2009). Lean philosophy in strategic supply chain management and value creating. *Journal of Global Strategic Management*, 5(1), p. 68.

Shah, R. & Ward, T. (2007). Defining and developing measures of lean production. *Journal of Operations Management*, 25(4), p. 785.

Slack, N., Chambers, S. & Johnson, R. (2010). *Operations Management*. Essex: Pitman Publishing.

Sterlacci, F. & Arbuckle, J. (2006). *Historical dictionaries of professions and industries 2*. Lanham, MD: Scarecrow Press.

Van Hoek, R. (1999). Postponement and the reconfiguration challenge for food supply chains. *Supply Chain Management: An International Journal*, 4(1), pp. 18–34.

White, R. & Pearson, J. (2001). JIT, system integration and customer service. *International Journal of Physical, Distribution & Logistics Management*, 31(5), pp. 313–333.

Womack, P., Jones, T. & Roos, D. (1990). *The Machine that Changed the World: The Story of Lean Production*. New York: Rawson Associates.

Wong, C. & Johansen, J. (2005). Making JIT retail a success: The coordination journey. *International Journal of Physical Distribution & Logistics Management*, 36(2), pp. 112–126.

Wu, T. & Blackhurst, J. (2009). *Managing supply chain risk and vulnerability: Tools and methods for supply chain decision makers*. London: Springer, pp. 37–38.

Yang, B. & Burns, N. (2003). Implications of postponement for the supply chain. *International Journal of Production Research*, 41(9), pp. 2075–2090.

Youssef, M. (1994). Agile manufacturing: The battle ground for competition in the 1990s and beyond. *International Journal of Operations Production Management*, 14(11), pp. 4–6.

Yusuf, Y.Y., Gunasekaran, A., Adeleye, E.O. & Sivayoganathan, K. (2004). Agile supply chain capabilities: Determinants of competitive objectives. *European Journal of Operational Research*, 159(2), pp. 379–392.

4

SUPPLY CHAIN INTEGRATION IN THE APPAREL INDUSTRY

4.1 Introduction

To deliver a product with the correct requirements is the forefront responsibility of any business and this importance is only magnified within the fashion apparel industry. It is becoming increasingly apparent to retailers that in order to compete, every aspect of the network needs to be examined and one problem many retailers face is how to best integrate their supply chain. Both vertical and horizontal integration act as solutions to the integration of this system, with both resolutions providing individual elements that cater for differing businesses.

Twenty years ago, 'global competition forced many manufacturing companies to improve the quality of their products and reduce their manufacturing costs' (Johnson & Pyke, 2001, p.8), which in turn, produced complications in determining the most efficient way to source their products. Due to this, apparel retailers felt the need to control this in a manner that meant that they had the upmost efficient control over the network. Consequently, in the late 1990s, the coordination of supply chain management 'finally began gaining momentum' (Johnson & Pyke, 2001). The momentum was triggered by external factors causing the retailers to respond. These external concerns present in the marketplace are all the more evident in the 21st century.

Within this increasingly competitive environment, it is known that 'the ultimate success of a single business will depend on management's ability to integrate the company's intricate network of business relationships' (Cooper & Lambert, 2000, p.1). Due to this, the 'conditions under which business is made are more turbulent' (Awad & Nassar, 2010, p.128), which is particularly relevant to the fashion sector, and the rapid rate at which it is happening has been highly publicised. Therefore, in the 21st century, it is a market requirement to get a higher-quality product/

service to the customer faster and more reliably than the competitor (Mentzer et al., 2007).

It is important to recognise and manage the integration challenges of the supply chain (Awad & Nassar, 2010). In order to integrate, the collaborative relationships happen within and beyond the business. Nowadays, firms 'are finding that they can no longer compete effectively in isolation of their suppliers or other entities in the supply chain' (Sandeep, 1998, p.31). These problems can be internal or external and it is the retailer's job to eradicate these complications by implementing solutions that best suit their business, giving them a competitive edge. Therefore, typically the goal is to create and coordinate manufacturing processes seamlessly across the supply chain in a manner that most competitors cannot easily match (Anderson & Katz, 1998; Lummus et al., 1998).

Supply chain integration is a 'key characteristic of Supply Chain Management' (Näslund & Hulthen, 2012, p.481), and it is therefore important that this topic is addressed in order to 'enhance process efficiency and effectiveness across members of the supply chain while creating value for their end-consumer' (Näslund & Hulthen, 2012, p.496). This integration includes the management of 'business, technology, people and processes not only within the enterprise, but also across extended enterprises' (Awad & Nassar, 2010, p.1), and is a vital component of a business due to the level of interdependency and coordination. With proven benefits, integrated supply chains result in lowered costs across the supply chain (Sundaram & Mehta, 2002). An integrated supply chain has full responsibility across the network and generally, the more synchronised and interconnected it is, the more successfully a business can perform. Although there are various solutions to problems surrounding integration, two of the most common solutions are vertical and horizontal integration.

4.2 Literature review

Integration has been commonly quoted as a key characteristic of supply chain management (Näslund & Hulthen, 2012). Supply chain management has been used to describe a number of concepts, from the purchasing and supplying within a dyadic relationship or holistically as the total chain of exchange from the original source of raw material, through its various processes and ultimately to the end consumer (Harland, 1997).

Supply chain integration became the subject of concern a number of years ago, regarding suppliers, manufacturers and customers (Frohlich & Westbrook, 2001). In highly competitive environments, such as apparel and garments, it is recognised as a strategy with a particular aim to improve business performance (Das & Narasimhan, 2001). This would agree with the view that integration has a single goal to 'enhance total process efficiency and effectiveness across members of the supply chain' (Lambert et al., 1998).

Over the years, technological advances have allowed businesses to integrate their supply chains more effectively, and effective integration of suppliers into the supply

46 Fashion supply chain integration

chain is a key factor for manufacturers in order to acquire the necessary competitive advantages needed in an increasingly competitive business environment (Ragatz et al., 2003). Theory has suggested for a long period of time that there is a need to integrate various internal functions (Hayes & Wheelwright, 1984), as well as the different functions/parties involved within the supply chain (Watts et al., 1995). Alongside this theory, there is 'empirical evidence' (Pagell, 2004) that integration of the specific internal functions, 'such as manufacturing and purchasing', will direct a business to higher performance (Das & Narasimhan, 2001).

The main factor causing the increased necessity of integration is globalisation. Most nations produce for the international textile and apparel market (Dickerson, 1995), making the apparel industry one of the most widespread industries with increasing links throughout the world. An increase in globalisation has led to a surge in the demand for product variety. Due to globalisation, the business environment has changed and has become more of a 'digital economy', which has impacted upon the supply chains of many businesses and therefore the need for effective communication is becoming increasingly imperative. Coordination amongst companies is becoming strategically important (D'Amours et al., 1999) within the current marketplace and this is also the case for coordination of the individual relationships within the business itself. For a company to strive, the market now demands more than just the act of simply delivering a product to store on time. Apparel businesses are competing in a market that requires 'sophisticated models to allocate production' (Johnson, 2006) in the most successful format for their company. Therefore, globalisation further enhances the demand for integrated supply chains, hence the need for it to be addressed as a significant supply chain management problem.

The increasing demand from consumers and from the current apparel market environment has led to a necessary need to control and manage a supply chain in an integrated manner. The two solutions proposed have been based on the fact that they are appropriate for the current disparity within the apparel market environment. Both vertical and horizontal integration individually provide the stability for companies that require different supply chain methods in order to successfully relay their products to their consumer market. It is important to note that the solution chosen is highly dependent upon the business itself and may differ due to differing requirements and demands.

4.3 Supply chain integration in the apparel industry

The apparel industry has developed a great deal through global sourcing and price competition. The industry has important market characteristics: low predictability, high volatility and a short product life cycle (Bruce et al., 2004), making ongoing decision making, based on research, difficult as there is little in terms of research and evidence to support any improvements made in the supply chain.

The textile and apparel industry will often have a long and complex supply chain with a number of parties involved (Jones, 2006). Such supply chains must be carefully managed in order to reduce the lead times to achieve the quick response needed (Bruce et al., 2004). In the apparel industry, differentiation advantages are built on brand images and product styling which can be quickly imitated, which can threaten to leave brands vulnerable (Richardson, 1996).

To support this need for effective management, integrative activities can be developed through different methods such as flow of goods, planning and control, organisation, and flow of information (Van Donk & Van der Vaart, 2005), and having the capacity to ensure the interconnectivity of the core business itself in relation to the other members of the apparel supply chain through elements such as geographical location, internal and external relationships, and supply chain activities.

Bowersox (1989) proposed that a supply chain should begin with the integration between supplier and consumer. This therefore includes both the internal business and the external environment working in harmony in order to communicate the desired information effectively. The importance of information technology within the integrative process and its impact upon each stage within a supply chain is therefore crucial. It also has specific importance within the apparel industry due to the constant need for both consumer and sales feedback in order to appropriately conduct future decisions. It has been known that information technology (IT) has been used in order to effectively integrate a supply chain through standardisation and information sharing through effective communication. For Spanish fast fashion retailer Zara, it is well publicised that supply chain management is the key to their corporate strategy (Stevenson, 2012), with their IT and communications being a main part of their success as an apparel retailer. IT has the capacity to work well as a solution for a more integrated apparel supply chain and it is important to state that one part of the supply chain cannot implement this solution in isolation and that for success, the communication of technology works best when all departments utilise this strategy in coordination with one another.

Specific factors said to have been previously used to integrate supply chain management include the control of transportation and logistics, outsourcing, IT, choice of location, and controlled inventory management. Due to 'rapid growth in third party logistics providers' (Johnson & Pyke, 2001, p.8) within the apparel business, there is a wide span of outsourcing logistics relationships that are important in maintaining a successfully integrated supply chain. Outsourcing decisions are vital to a business's success and the growth of the apparel sector only means there is 'a large and expanding group of technologies and services to be examined' (Johnson & Pyke, 2001, p.9). Outsourcing is used in apparel businesses successfully in order to integrate their supply chain and has specific connections within India and China (Johnson, 2006). The use of both outsourcing and IT in particular are examples of alternative solutions to form an integrated supply chain network.

4.4 Vertical integration

An enterprise is vertically integrated along a supply chain when it owns assets (Grossman & Hart, 1986), organises activities or controls activities both upstream and downstream (Aoki et al., 1990; Richardson, 1996). Vertical integration has not been considered to be a superior form of retailer in particularly volatile environments; however, there are some market characteristics found in the apparel industry that could prove to be advantageous to implementing rapid response (Richardson, 1996).

A number of companies have employed strategies such as quick response and accurate response to improve their supply chains (Chandra & Kumar, 2000), whilst it is also common for a just-in-time strategy to be implemented. Quick response is a strategy that most accurately describes the alignment of design, retail and manufacturing operations that will present the flexibility to respond to constantly changing markets (Hammond, 1990). Quick response then leads to such benefits as reduced inventory costs, fewer markdowns of overproduced items, and occasionally increased sales of popular items (Richardson, 1996).

The current environment emphasises timing and know-how: vertically integrated companies have been able to benefit from innovations and quick response, which are designed to shorten the potentially lengthy production cycle (Richardson, 1996). By using their quick response and utilising technology, these organisations are able to evolve their capabilities in terms of learning, communication and coordination, allowing them to try out designs and products, imitating others and then continuing to produce those that sell.

Vertically integrated firms have begun to link their quick response into retailing and these firms are able to demonstrate possession of the necessary elements of retailer that in turn allow them to be flexible and fast, whilst understanding the demand and customer satisfaction need. Pagell (2004, p.459) states that 'a lack of integration indicates processes working at cross-purposes leading to lower levels of organizational performance', suggesting that the importance of integration is undoubtedly crucial to success.

Some studies have found that vertical integration could create a concrete obligation to assets and capabilities that could be vulnerable to value loss if the market circumstances were to change considerably (Teece, 1992). 'Extensive vertical integration is probably a liability in industries with volatile structure' (Harrigan, 1983, p.401), as it will most likely cause a limit in flexibility and insulate the retailer so that it is unable to gain information about both the input and product markets. This was further supported by a further study (D'Aveni & Ilinitch, 1992), which found that the ability of a retailer to adapt to environmental turmoil is reduced by complex vertical integration, which consequently increases risk.

However, as previously mentioned, there are some potential benefits to vertical integration in the apparel industry. Harrigan (1983) found that such integration provides product differentiation advantages along with marketing intelligence; in apparel these are significant factors and elements of the business. Although such studies may be true, it has been pointed out that organisational flexibility is relative to the market demands and should therefore be matched accordingly (Volberda, 1996). Harrigan developed a series of classifying types of organisational flexibility and includes conditions by which each is most suited. It could be seen that vertical integration 'provides apparel firms with superior operational flexibility to achieve quick response, but could also constrain structural or strategic flexibility' (Richardson, 1996, p.403).

4.5 Horizontal integration

A business becomes horizontally integrated when it 'expands with a business at the same point within the supply chain, either within the same industry or a different one' (Mitzsheva, 2014, p.2). The goal is to achieve effective and efficient flows of products and services, information, along with money and decisions to provide maximum value to the customer at a lower cost and higher speed (Frohlich & Westbrook, 2001).

A framework produced by Bower distinguishes three main areas of impact within the supply chain, which include resources, processes and values. Resources include both tangible and intangible assets, processes such as the activities the firms use to turn resources into goods and services, and the values that underpin the decisions that the employees make (Bower, 2001).

Integrating horizontally through mergers and acquisitions has become an inseparable part of business internationally and a major means for firms to grow, become international or obtain know-how. Firms now more frequently use mergers in order to increase sales and profit. However, in the 1960s the motive to create a merger was to build a conglomerate (Lotta, 2004).

Only recently has there been an increase in a call for a systematic approach towards the integration of supply chains. This is due to increasingly global competition that has caused organisations to rethink the need and possibility of mutually beneficial supply chain partnerships (Lambert & Cooper, 2000), and the priority surrounding joint improvement of inter-organisational processes has become higher (Zhao et al., 2008).

However, the majority of mergers and acquisitions have actually proven to result in a decrease in shareholder value (Brews, 2000). The largest horizontal deal in both the sport and footwear industry was the merger between Adidas and Reebok in 2005, which witnessed Adidas' technology knowledge and Reebok's sales performance and goals as a good match. However, observers commented that there were too many product and market overlaps to make it work successfully (Perkins & Anh Vu, 2009). The Adidas Group in 2005 stated that the brands would be kept separate because each brand has a lot of value and it would be stupid to bring them both together. Instead, the company would continue selling their products under their own, respective brand names and labels.

According to Thomson Financial, in the first nine months of 2007 worldwide merger activity hit US$3.6 billion, surpassing the total from all 2006 combined (Wong, 2007). Integrating horizontally through collaboration within transport management is proposed to overcome some inherent inefficiency, providing a superior winning performance (Mason et al., 2007). On the other hand, future competition is said to be between supply chain networks rather than between companies (De Souza et al., 2000).

4.6 Analysis of the two solutions

Integrating within the supply chain horizontally introduces a number of benefits to a company as they are introduced to a further spread of markets through merger and acquisition of other firms. As a firm becomes larger through horizontal integration they reap benefits from economies of scale as they start to buy raw materials in

50 Fashion supply chain integration

much bigger bulk and benefit from much lower long-run average costs, resulting in lower costs overall which allow them to become much more efficient. Both merging with and taking over different companies allows companies to become much more diverse within the product range and services which they offer so they can appeal and cater for a larger market. Once a firm grows they become much more dominant within the market and gain more market power. This can be especially beneficial when negotiating deals with suppliers and distributors as they are more powerful and may be able to dictate a less expensive price and can therefore benefit from more overall profit.

Becoming more powerful within the market also allows a company to dominate customers over price, due to the fact that customers are still bound to purchase a product for a higher price due to the unavailability of similar products as competing firms have lost their share in the market. For example, one apparel company which uses horizontal integration is Gap Inc. By acquiring a number of different brands they have been able to appeal to and cater for a much wider and diverse market offering fast, throwaway fashion to more high-quality goods to last longer across their portfolio of brands; however, with vertical integration this can be much more difficult. Through the acquisitions they have made, they have been able to increase their market share and become more dominant within the markets to which they cater.

When increasing market share through horizontal integration there becomes less competition in the market where firms can benefit from a much less intense trading environment and become the more dominant member of the competition within the industry. Unlike horizontal integration, integrating vertically will have no impact on limiting the competition as existing competition will still exist. Horizontal integration can often include integrating with firms abroad in the same industry who offer similar products and services. This allows companies to grow through increased access to new markets where they can make their products more knowledgeable and increase interest. This also allows the cost of international trade to be reduced as less costly mistakes are often made and the knowledge of the other firm belonging to the merger of the international country is often very profitable.

Merging with different companies allows rationalisation to take place where costs savings can be made through having to employ fewer workers, managers and premises as both firms begin to integrate. Economies of scope can also be gained through horizontal integration where a cost advantage can be made when producing two or more products where companies can share the resources. This allows the firms to spread out the costs resulting in fewer costs for each company whilst increasing the amount of products they promote at the same cost. It also allows for distribution costs to be reduced as these can be spread out also.

References

Anderson, M.G. & Katz, P.B. (1998). Strategic Sourcing. *International Journal of Logistics Management*, 9(1), pp. 1–13.

Aoki, M., Gustafsson, B. & Williamson, O.E. (1990). *The Firm as a Nexus of Treaties* (Advanced Studies in the Social Sciences), 1st edn. New York: Sage Publications.

Awad, H.A.H. & Nassar, M.O. (2010). Supply Chain Integration: Definition and Challenges. *International MultiConference of Engineers and Computer Scientists*, 1.

Bower, J.L. (2001). Not all M&As are Alike – and That Matters. *Harvard Business Review*, 2, March, pp. 93–101.

Bowersox, D.J. (1989). Logistics in the integrated enterprise. *Proceedings of the Annual Conference of the Council of Logistics Management*, St Louis, MO.

Brews, P.J. (2000). The Challenge of the Web-Enabled Business. *Financial Times*, 24 November.

Bruce, M., Daly, M. & Towers, N. (2004). Lean or agile: A solution for supply chain management in the textiles and clothing industry? *International Journal of Operations & Production Management*, 24(2), pp. 151–170.

Chandra, C. & Kumar, S. (2000). An application of a system analysis methodology to manage logistics in a textile supply chain. *Supply Chain Management, An International Journal*, 5(5), pp. 234–244.

Cooper, M.C. & Lambert, D.M. (2000). Issues in Supply Chain Management. *Industrial Marketing Management*, 29, pp. 65–83.

D'Amours, S., Montreuil, B., Lefrancois., P. & Soumis, F. (1999). Networked Manufacturing: The impact of information sharing. *International Journal of Production Economics*, 58, pp. 63–79.

Das, A. & Narasimhan, R. (2001). The impact of purchasing integration and practices on manufacturing performance. *Journal of Operations Management*, 19(5), pp. 593–609.

D'Aveni, R.A. & Ilinitch, A.Y. (1992). Complex Patterns of Vertical Integration in the Forest Products Industry: Systematic and Bankruptcy Risks. *The Academy of Management Journal*, 35(3), pp. 596–625.

De Souza, R., Zice, S. & Chaoyang, L. (2000). Supply chain dynamics and optimization. *Integrated Manufacturing Systems*, 11(5), pp. 348–364.

DeWitt, W., Keebler, J.S., Mentzer, J.T., Min, S., Nix, N.W., Smith, C.D. & Zacharia, Z. G. (2007). Defining Supply Chain Management. *Journal of Business Logistics*, 22(2).

Dickerson, Kitty G. (1995). *Textiles and apparel in the global economy*, 2nd edn. Englewood Cliffs, NJ: Prentice Hall.

Economic Expert (n.d.). Horizontal Integration [online]. Available at: www.economicexpert. com/a/Horizontal:integration.htm [accessed 19 April 2014].

Flynn, Barbara B., Huo, Baofeng & Zhao, Xiande (2010). The impact of supply chain integration on performance: A contingency and configuration approach. *Journal of Operations Management*, 28(1), pp. 58–71.

Frohlich, M.T. & Westbrook, R. (2001). Arcs of integration: An international study of supply chain strategies. *Journal of Operations Management*, 19(2), pp. 185–200.

Grossman, S.J. & Hart, O.D. (1986). The Costs and Benefits of Ownership: A Theory of Vertical and Lateral Integration. *Journal of Political Economy*, 94(4), pp. 691–719.

Häkkinen, L. (2004). Mergers and Acquisitions in the Logistics Service Industry: Case Study Findings, Conference Proceedings. *Proceedings of the Second IASTED International Conference Alliances, Mergers and Acquisitions*, Cambridge, pp. 158–168.

Häkkinen, Lotta, Norman, Andreas, Hilmola, Olli-Pekka & Ojala, Lauri (2004). Logistics Integration in Horizontal Mergers and Acquisitions. *The International Journal of Logistics Management*, 15(1), pp. 27–42.

Hammond, J.H. (1990). *Quick Response in the Apparel Industry*. Cambridge: Harvard Business School.

Harland, C. (1997). Supply chain operational performance roles. *Journal of Manufacturing Technology Management*, 8(2), pp. 70–78.

Harrigan, K.R. (1983). *Strategies for Vertical Integration*, 1st edn. Lexington: Lexington Books.

Hayes, R.H. & Wheelwright, S.C. (1984). *Restoring Our Competitive Edge: Competing Through Manufacturing*, 1st edn. New York: Wiley.

Johnson, E.M. (2006). Supply Chain Management: Technology, Globalization, and Policy at a Crossroad. *Interfaces*, 36(3), pp. 191–193.

Johnson, E.M. & Pyke, D.F. (2001). Supply Chain Management: Integration and Globalization in the Age of eBusiness. *Manufacturing Engineering Handbook*, p. 8.

Jones, R.M. (2006). *The Apparel Industry*, 2nd edn. New York: John Wiley & Sons.

Jurevicius, O. (2013). Horizontal integration: Definition, examples, advantages. *Strategic Management Insight* [online]. Available at: www.strategicmanagementinsight.com/topics/horizontal-integration.html [accessed 19 April 2014].

Lambert, D.M. & Cooper, M.C. (2000). Issues in supply chain management. *Industrial Marketing Management*, 29(1), pp. 65–83.

Lambert, D.M., Cooper, M.C. & Pagh, J.D. (1998). Supply Chain Management: Implementation Issues and Research Opportunities. *The International Journal of Logistics Management*, 9(2), pp. 1–20.

Lummus, R.R., Vokurka, R.J. & Alber, K.L. (1998). Strategic Supply Chain Planning. *Production and Inventory Management Journal*, 39(3), pp. 49–58.

Mason, Robert, Lalwani, Chandra & Boughton, Roger (2007). Combining vertical and horizontal collaboration for transport optimisation. *Supply Chain Management: An International Journal*, 12(3), pp. 187–199.

Mentzer, J.T., Myers, M.B. & Stank, T.P. (2007). *Handbook of Global Supply Chain Management*. USA: Sage Publications, Inc.

Mitzsheva, M. (2014). Definition of Horizontal Integration in a Supply Chain [online]. Available at: http://smallbusiness.chron.com/definition-horizontal-integration-supply-chain-34736.html [accessed 20 April 2014].

Nagurney, A., Woolley, T. & Qiang, Q. (2010). Multi-product supply chain horizontal network integration: Models, theory, and computational results. *International Transactions in Operational Research*, 17(3), pp. 333–349.

Näslund, D. & Hulthen, H. (2012). Supply chain management integration: A critical analysis. *Benchmarking: An International Journal*, 19(4/5), pp. 481–501.

Pagell, M. (2004). Understanding the factors that enable and inhibit the integration of operations, purchasing and logistics. *Journal of Operations Management*, 22(5), pp. 459–487.

Perkins, D.H. & Anh Vu, T.T. (2009). *Vietnam's Industrial Policy. Designing Policies for Sustainable Development*. Policy Dialogue Paper 1, prepared under the UNDP – Harvard Policy Dialogue Papers Series on Vietnam's WTO Accession and International Competitiveness Research. Cambridge, MA: Harvard University.

Ragatz, G.L., Handfield, R.B. & Scannell, T.V. (2003). Success Factors for Integrating Suppliers into New Product Development. *Journal of Product Innovation Management*, 14(3) (2 October), pp. 190–201.

Richardson, J. (1996). Vertical Integration and Rapid Response in Fashion Apparel. *Organization Science*, 7(4), pp. 400–412.

Sandeep, P. (1998). ERP and Web-based self-service. *Computing Canada*, 24(42).

Singh, S. (n.d.). Advantages and Disadvantages of Horizontal Integration [online]. Available at: www.ehow.co.uk/info_8444143_advantages-disadvantages-horizontal-integration.html [accessed 19 April 2014].

Stevenson, S. (2012). Zara's Fast Fashion. *Slate* [online]. Available at: www.slate.com/articles/arts/operations/2012/06/zara_s_fast_fashion_how_the_company_gets_new_styles_to_stores_so_quickly_.html [accessed 9 April 2014].

Sundaram, R.M. & Mehta, S.G. (2002). A comparative study of three SCM approaches. *International Journal of Physical Distribution & Logistics Management*, 32(7), pp. 532–555.

Teece, D.J. (1992). Competition, cooperation, and innovation: Organizational arrangements for regimes of rapid technological progress. *Journal of Economic Behaviour and Organization*, 18(1), pp. 1–25.

Van der Vaart, T. & Van Donk, D.P. (2004). Buyer focus: Evaluation of a new concept for supply chain integration. *International Journal of Production Economics*.

Van Donk, D.P. & Van der Vaart, T. (2005). 'A Critical Discussion on the Theoretical and Methodological Advancements in Supply Chain Integration Research', in H. Kotzab, S. Seuring, M. Müller & G. Reiner (eds), *Research Methodologies in Supply Chain Management*. Physica-Verlag H.

Volberda, H.W. (1996). Toward the Flexible Form: How to Remain Vital in Hypercompetitive Environments. *Organizational Science*, 7(4), p. 35937.

Vu, Dung Anh, Shi, Yongjiang & Hanby, Terry (2009). Strategic framework for brand integration in horizontal mergers and acquisitions. *Journal of Technology Management in China*, 4(1), pp. 26–52.

Wang, W.Y.C. & Chan, H.K. (2010). Virtual organization for supply chain integration: Two cases in the textile and fashion retailing industry. *International Journal of Production Economics*, 127(2), pp. 333–342.

Watts, C.A., Kim, K.Y. & Hahn, C.K. (1995). Linking Purchasing to Corporate Competitive Strategy. *Journal of Supply Chain Management*, 31(1), pp. 2–8.

Wong, P.T.P. (2007). 'Positive psychology and a positive revolution', in P.T.P. Wong, M. McDonald & D. Klaassen (eds), *The Positive Psychology of Meaning and Spirituality*. Abbotsford, BC: INPM Press.

Zhao, S., Grasmuck, S. & Martin, J. (2008). Identity Construction on Facebook: Digital Empowerment in Anchored Relationships. *Computers in Human Behavior*, 24(5), pp. 1816–1836.

5

FASHION SUPPLY CHAIN TRACEABILITY

RFID vs barcode

5.1 Introduction

Traceability is a core issue within the fashion industry due to the complexity of the apparel pipeline. Indeed customers' demands are continuously changing. The aim of this chapter is to study the traceability of products within the fashion supply chain. This chapter will introduce two different ways to trace goods: barcodes and radio frequency identification (RFID). It will focus on identifying advantages and disadvantages of the two technologies and analysing critically their applications in real businesses.

The quick expansion of fast fashion brands like Zara and H&M is described as 'the speed of fashion' according to the professionals' words. The word 'speed' does not only refer to the rapid development of these fashion retailers, it is also used to characterise their responsive agile supply chain. Thus supply chain management (SCM) is one of the key success factors and has many parties involved. Whether an organisation can approach suitable solutions to trace and track the information, goods and services flow from beginning of procurement to end consumer, is a critical part of the company's success. This kind of ability is defined as 'traceability'.

Over the past decades, in the textile apparel pipeline, localised production networks have increasingly lost their advantage due to newly industrialised countries and emerging markets such as the Far East where there are low production costs. Therefore, Guercini's (n.d.) article points out that traceability will be the increasing need to solve the problem in global supply chains caused by geographic distance. Consequently, traceability is used to manage a global production network. He also explains that traceability's main role is to be a tool for inter-organisational control. Indeed, it allows understanding of how each operation participates in the supply chain and contributes. Through systemic methods of identification a company, hence, can use the result to analyse the contribution of different stages and make decisions. In addition, Palmer (1995) has a similar opinion but divides 'control' into more detail. He includes optimisation of the products' quality and process, better control of production and logistics operations, in order to increase efficiency and reach consistency. Moreover, in the fashion industry the clothes have a short product life cycle (PLC) and trends, customers' needs change so fast that brands have to be responsive, which is currently defined as quick response (QR).

Since traceability is a key issue, 'how to enhance traceability of a business in fashion apparel by developing systematic solutions for its supply chain' will be the problem to be discussed in this chapter.

5.2 Barcodes

Barcodes 'are printed horizontal strips of vertical bars used for identifying specific items', and a 'scanning device reads the barcode by moving a beam across the symbol' (Grieco, 1989, p.16). From its invention in 1932 until today, barcodes have proven reliable performers especially in fashion retailing. An article written by Seideman (2011) gives a relevant description of the period before barcodes were invented and a comparison between tracing the supply chain by pure manpower or a system. Another article, written by McCathie (2004), assesses a wide range of advantages and disadvantages of barcode system. It points out that the barcode system is mature and has been widely used in retail for a long time. Thus, there is no risk to implementing that system. Meanwhile, the investment and maintenance costs of barcodes are low. Some examples like 'Alto Group hits high notes with new inventory management system' and 'RF cuts processing time for Lexus car and parts deliveries' (*Automatic I.D. News Asia*, 1998a, 1998b), provide an analysis of how barcode technology is helping companies to improve their SCM. Although these cases are not relevant to the apparel industry, they are still good evidence to prove barcodes are useful.

However, barcodes also have weaknesses. The article written by Russell (2010) explains that barcodes are a graphic image featuring a series of lines or bars positioned parallel to each other, in such a way scanners need a direct line of sight and close quarters to read the barcode, which consequently reduces the efficiency. Furthermore, Russell (2010) points out that barcodes only have limited storage capacities; they only can contain a few English letters and numerals. Besides, Herand's (2014) article talks about the innovation of barcodes nowadays, in 2D (two-dimensional) barcodes, also named the QR code.

FIGURE 5.1 Sample Bar code

56 Fashion supply chain traceability

By inheriting all the advantages of the original system, the QR code has developed more. Its reading speed is 30% faster than a classic barcode and it contains more information – up to 512KB. A case study by Lambert (2011) is talking about Adidas adding QR codes to their labels.

The stability and sustainability of barcodes involve a low risk of implementing this system and its cost is low. By offering enhancement of traceability in a low-cost way, it encourages all businesses to use it. This encourages each actor along the supply chain to use it, from upstream to downstream. Then, it is easy to use this system to communicate with suppliers and customers and to have integrated information on traceability. Nevertheless, except for the traditional barcode, the QR code is increasingly applied by industry. The large storage of data enables it to be closely combined with smartphones and mobile internet, which will be a huge potential market in the future. Hence, implementing a QR code system might be a strategic issue for many companies.

However, every system has its weaknesses. Regarding barcodes, the most serious drawback in textile industry is that they are easily smeared, smudged or damaged, since they have to be printed outside the garments. This will cause additional scanning problems, due to illegible reading of the barcode; the checkout process can be significantly delayed while another package of the same merchandise is located and brought to the checkout counter for scanning (Bogan & Callahan, 2001). Thus, barcodes reduce the value that suppliers provide to consumers. In other words, it decreases the value creation of SCM, a result of inefficient services which waste consumers' time. Moreover, it is impossible to scan the barcode if it is damaged. Therefore, the lifetime of a barcode is short and it cannot be reused, leading to a discommodity in long-term SCM.

Barcodes have to be scanned individually which results in intensive labour. Furthermore, the storage capacity of barcodes is limited, in such a way that it only presents the information of manufacturers and products, and therefore cannot read or write any added information. For instance, the information about the quality of the products cannot be shown during the process of scanning; in this case, consumers may only gain the information on products by asking a shop assistant, and the shop assistant has to find the information on computer after scanning the product, which makes the SCM inefficient. Low security is also one of the undesirable points of the barcode, because it is easy to reproduce or to forge a barcode. For example, some manufacturers use registered codes of other manufacturers in order to constitute a new barcode for their own products, which deceives consumers.

Although the barcode has several disadvantages it is used by many fashion retailers, such as Primark, New Look and Topshop. Nevertheless, RFID technology has been growing for some years.

5.3 RFID

A newer technology, RFID, has appeared recently replacing barcodes gradually along the supply chain. It is a technology that uses tiny computer chips to track items such as consumer commodities at a distance. This solution is being increasingly appreciated by the apparel industry. A large amount of literature, about the advantages and disadvantages offered by this technology, has been published over the last decades. The main purpose is to understand which benefits fashion companies could get by implementing RFID instead of barcodes.

First and foremost, Moon and Ngai (2008) explain in their report what RFID contains: it is a tag made of an antenna, a conductor chip attached to this one and a form of encapsulation around it. They also describe that the reader is responsible for powering and communicating data with the tag. According to their report, the RFID working principle was discovered in 1940 and was even used by the British during World War II. This technology remained relatively obscure for years but nowadays it is experiencing a true revival, especially in the apparel industry thanks to the numerous advantages it offers to retailers.

Indeed, an article written by Wamba (2012) points out the positive features of RFID technology. Compared to a barcode, the reading process is completely different; several products can be scanned at a time. Moreover, there is no visibility required and the distance of reading is high. The data storage capability of a tag is huge and it can be reused. Besides, the user can add and modify information at any time. Furthermore, the tag itself is protected in a plastic case which makes it rugged and resistant to the environment. Last, Moon and Ngai (2008) point out that RFID involves electronics and informatics systems allowing an almost inexistent error rate. Much of the literature demonstrates the benefits of RFID implementation, but this technology has also many disadvantages.

Firstly, the price of a tag, even if it tends to decrease, is relatively higher than a barcode, as Kwok and Wu (2009) explain in their report. Implementing this technology along the supply chain is therefore an important investment for a company. Besides, according to Azvedo and Carvalho's (2012, p.132) research, 'RFID technology involves a substantial investment […] this type of technology has a high level of obsolescence and innovation'. Because of the high cost of

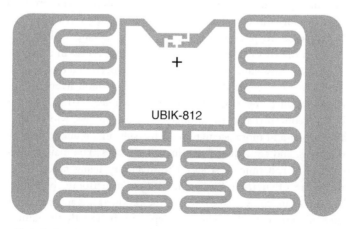

FIGURE 5.2 Sample RFID tag (ESRL-812)

58 Fashion supply chain traceability

RFID, some fashion companies are reluctant to implement it along their supply chain, thinking that a new technology or an improvement in RFID could appear in a few years. In addition, ABI Research (2009) points out the consumer privacy issues related to the use of RFID tags. Indeed, RFID can be used for tracking and understanding consumer behaviour, which is nowadays controversial. In that way, ABI Research's article explains that some rules have being established in the European Union to inform customers of the presence of RFID tags on their products, although most retailers do not follow the rules. According to Moon and Ngai (2008), it contributes a serious brake on the implementation of this technology.

Moreover, Charikleia (2010) indicates that the main weakness of the technology is that companies must equip the whole supply chain with the RFID system with a common standard. According to Kwok and Wu (2009), the implementation could, therefore, be long and expensive. Charikleia's (2010) article goes further by explaining that a company could face interference issues between different radio frequencies. The causes of these defects are related to the components of RFID technology.

As described in Charikleia's (2010) article, the frequency of RFID technology is classified by low frequency (125–135 kHz), high frequency (HF 13.56 MHz), ultra-high frequency (UHF 860–960 MHz), and super-high frequency (2.446–2.454 GHz), which all have their own different read range. HF and UHF are the two main types of radio frequencies applied by the readers. Lastly, Kwok and Wu (2009) discussed health issues which could be caused by the radio waves from the RFID tags. This disadvantage explains partly consumers' reluctance.

On the whole, the literature points out that both barcodes and RFID can be used as a relevant system to trace products along the supply chain. Nevertheless, they also provide additional and different benefits for a fashion retailer linked to its activities. The choice between the two technologies depends on several factors. Before talking about these factors, it is important to focus on barcodes and RFID in the fashion industry and to compare them.

RFID technology can occur on every step of the supply chain, from suppliers to final customers going through distribution centre and shops (Moon & Ngai, 2008). Indeed, RFID tags are put on all clothes, cases and ranges. This involves data sharing between the partners and trusting them to use RFID in an efficient way.

Firstly, the main advantage of RFID concerns its speed in terms of inventory and delivery lead time. Indeed, it allows better control of the delivery and order picking, and most of all better stock management (Wamba, 2012). For instance, the labour force is reduced thanks to automation of the process. Moreover the inventory is faster, easier and more accurate, which results in a reduction in out-of-stock (OOS) situations, and consequently an increase in sales. The main goal of RFID is the knowledge in real time of stock. The inventory being faster, then it can be carried out more often (ABI Research, 2009). Furthermore, by using RFID in shops, the sellers can know exactly where the products are and react immediately. For instance, if a product is sold they can replace it by exactly the same or another one on the shop floor preventing thus the OOS and missing sales (GS1 Memove,

2012). At last, the checkout can be equipped with RFID readers allowing the scanning of all the products in one basket at a time, consequently avoiding queues (GS1 Memove, 2012). As a source of innovation, it will maybe change the organisation of shops, like intelligent ones or emergence of smart fitting rooms that suggest items such as accessories or clothes that go well with the chosen product (GS1 Memove, 2012). Another main advantage of RFID concerns theft and counterfeiting prevention. In fact, the information cannot be replicated and can be secured, preventing thieves and reproduction (Moon & Ngai, 2008).

However, RFID also faces a number of implementation challenges, the main one being the cost and consequently the return on investment (ROI). The high cost of implementation is a brake in the spread of RFID. According to an ARC Advisory Group survey in 2004, over half of the companies interviewed do not expect a quick ROI after applying RFID technology. However, some successful companies had an ROI between 6 to 12 months (ABI Research, 2009). In addition, most of the workers and suppliers do not know how to use this technology, so companies should spend time to train them, causing additional costs. As explained in the literature review, other disadvantages exist such as privacy and health issues or frequency interference. For example, JC Penney, a US fashion retailer, started to implement RFID in 2012. At the outset, the company was faced with wave interference problems between the radio signal emitted by RFID anti-theft tags. The brand decided to remove the anti-theft tags but an increase in the theft of products was noticed, causing lost profits of $28 million.

Unable to find a solution, JC Penney scrapped the project in 2013 (*Supply Chain Digest*, 2013). However, other retailers found a solution to this issue, like Zara. Learning from its competitors' mistakes, Zara launched a reusable tag. Chips are placed inside the security alarm, in a plastic bag and are removed during the checkout. The recovery of tags is a benefit for reducing cost by reusing chips and also for avoiding problems concerning privacy of customers.

RFID and barcodes have both advantages and disadvantages for a fashion retailer. In order to make a decision between the two technologies, it is necessary to analyse which similarities and differences exist between them.

5.4 Similarities between the two solutions

The two solutions for traceability are similar in a number of points. First of all they are used to identify products and the principle is to incorporate an object (barcode or RFID) on clothes or more generally on products. Moreover, the system enables the reading of encrypted data. It is used to improve traceability of products and have better control of production, products and stocks. So as to be efficient, the system must be involved in each stage of the supply chain.

The main differences are discussed based on the functioning of the solutions. First of all, unlike barcodes, it's possible to read several RFID tags at a time. Then, a visual contact is needed to read a barcode whereas a large distance is possible for

60 Fashion supply chain traceability

an RFID. The storage capacity varies and is much more important for RFID than for barcodes. Indeed, an RFID tag can carry more than 256 bits whereas a barcode can only contain until 50 bits (Blecker & Huang, 2008). By contrast, some problems appear with the utilisation of RFID such as the non-protection of privacy, which could be controversial, and the wave's interference that can restrain the reading of RFID tag data. Barcodes and RFID help to fight against counterfeiting and theft by identifying uniquely each product, but barcodes are easy to reproduce.

Moreover, RFID can be used as an anti-theft device contrary to barcodes. The price is also different. Indeed, a barcode costs on average $1, whereas an RFID tag costs on average $10, although some can be found at a lower price if the storage capacity is low (ABI Research, 2009). RFID tags have great resistance and can have a ten-year life span, while barcodes can be deleted with time. Regarding the two solutions, RFID can be reused as data can be updated at any time, contrary to barcodes that are of single use. One of the major benefits of RFID is the time saved during inventory. For example, for the same amount of items, an inventory using barcodes takes 53 hours whereas with RFID it takes only 2 hours (ABI Research, 2009). This implicates a decreased need of human labour and the possibility of increasing frequency of inventory. These differences are very important for a company because it can save time and money and gain accuracy.

Faced with the numerous advantages of RFID, some companies tried to implement this technology in their supply chain. Some companies succeeded, others had to stop for various reasons. Using the technology as a competitive advantage could then become a wrong brand strategy. Finally the choice between RFID and barcodes is not that simple and depends on several factors. In that way, the company has to undertake a deep analysis to compare which is the most relevant and profitable method for its business.

Table 5.1 summarises the controlling factors that need to be considered for the choice between the two technologies.

First of all, the implementation of RFID is easier when the brand is vertically integrated. It means that the firm owns manufacturers and every stakeholder while with horizontal integration suppliers are independent. The brand does not have to face suppliers' issues, but only convince them to use RFID in their factories and distribution centres, as Marks & Spencer did. Indeed, as mentioned above, the cost

TABLE 5.1 The choice between RFID and barcodes depends on several factors

Factors	Barcodes	RFID
Integration (ABI Research, 2009)	Horizontal	Vertical
Loop (ABI Research, 2009; Cronin, 2009)	Open-loop	Closed-loop
Brand strategy (Moon & Ngai, 2008)	High fashion	Fast fashion – brand image – customer service
Volume/diversity (Kwok & Wu, 2009, p.4)	Low	High
Bargaining power (Balocco et al., 2011, p.12)	Minimum	Maximum

of RFID tags is very high compared to barcodes. Most suppliers that have used barcodes for a long time refuse to invest in RFID because they will not benefit from it (Balocco et al., 2011).

Walmart is not a fashion retailer but its analysis is interesting because it was one of the first big retailers that used RFID in its supply chain. Indeed, in 2003, the company decided to impose this technology to its top 100 suppliers. Three years later, more than 600 suppliers were involved in the project, not expecting any profits but hoping for a better relationship with Walmart. However, a lot of suppliers still had difficulty in implementing RFID into their system. Then, in order to put pressure on them, Walmart chose to create a $2 fee for every supplier delivering a case without RFID tags on the products. Major suppliers then reconsidered their collaboration with Walmart due to the high costs involved in RFID. Walmart finally decided to remove this fee (Balocco et al., 2011). By contrast, Zara is working in a vertical integration. In 2012, the brand decided to implement RFID in stores. The group owns its factories and controls all the manufacturing process, thus it has not had to face suppliers' issues, contrary to Walmart (Bjork, 2014). Finally, working in vertical integration allows retailers to implement RFID more easily with no sharing profits (Balocco et al., 2011), which explains the success of Zara, unlike Walmart.

5.5 Open- or closed-loop system

Another factor for a company to consider is the selection of an open-loop or closed-loop system. Closed loop means that the RFID tag is continuously recycled along the supply chain process. In this way, the cost of the tag is amortised and has a good cost-efficiency ratio. Retailers have more control along the supply chain as the firm is the only one coordinating the flow (Hellström & Wiberg, 2010). There are fewer logistical issues (standardisation of the software) and no information is shared with suppliers (Cronin, 2009). All these reasons make the closed loop the first system used by brands willing to implement RFID (ABI Research, 2009).

In an open-loop system, 'the collaboration between business partners is critical to success' (ABI Research, 2009). Indeed, in this case, the RFID-tagged item passes from manufacturer, to distributor, and to retailer in an integrated network with information shared between them. More and more retailers begin to operate in an open loop with RFID but this involves costs and trust in your partners. If a brand does not operate in a close-loop system, it could be more difficult and more expensive to introduce the RFID technology.

RFID is expensive for a fashion retailer and turns out not to be relevant according to the brand strategy. In fact, RFID is useful for large retailers that deal with a wide product range in terms of sizes, styles and colours in order to improve its inventory accuracy (Moon, 2008). It is often the case for fast fashion retailers, like Zara, which offers products with a short product life cycle, for which QR is the key to success (Moon, 2008). However, if products are cheap, such as Primark's commodities, the tag cost could be higher than the goods value and then

62 Fashion supply chain traceability

barcodes remain a better alternative (Zetes, 2009). On the contrary, small retailers or/and luxury brands do not need to manage a huge amount of goods, data and sales but only low volumes. Barcodes could thus be the appropriate solution to handle the stock (Moon, 2008). However, RFID could offer a competitive advantage by improving customer service, essential for high-end brands.

For instance, American Apparel is the most important retailer in the USA. Its strategy is to offer products in every size and colour at any time in store to satisfy customers' needs. Thus, American Apparel is a perfect candidate for the RFID. It began to use the technology in 2007 by tagging more than 40,000 items. The year after, it improved its sales by 14% per store, the accuracy of inventory by 99%, and saved around 190 hours of labour per store. The company spent less than $50,000 to equip its stores and had an ROI in only five months (ABI Research, 2009). One unique solution does not exist and criteria to use RFID instead of barcodes depend on the brand strategy.

Barcodes are the most widely used in the fashion supply chain. Thus, if fashion retailers want to introduce RFID, they must have a strong influence to persuade their suppliers to implement RFID in their systems, as seen in the Walmart case. RFID is obviously a good way for a fashion retailer to differentiate itself from its competitors by increasing its inventory accuracy and being more responsive. However, it cannot be the best solution, involving more expenditure than profit, especially for small retailers with a small product range. Finally, each company willing to implement RFID has to undertake a deep analysis before making a decision.

5.6 Summary

Traceability is very important in the textile and apparel industry because of the huge flow of products. Indeed, products are often renewed with the emergence of fast fashion, so faster and more accurate inventory is needed. The barcode technology is currently the most used in the retail industry because of its low cost and its democratisation that allows companies to work in harmony with suppliers and customers. But barcodes are not the most precise solution and human mistakes can happen. The RFID technology enables quick and accurate inventory, can be used both in the supply chain and in stores for better customer service. But the cost of the system is important and to be more efficient it is necessary to implement the technology in the whole supply chain. That is why a company needs to undertake a deep analysis upstream before choosing this solution. There is no one best solution; it really depends on the characteristics of the company in question, and finally similarities enable the two solutions to be used in conjunction.

A fashion retailer can make a profit from RFID by reducing its labour costs, its OOS, increasing sales and also improving customer service. This technology offers several advantages along the supply chain such as a better inventory accuracy, better control of the retail process and finally logistics optimisation. However, it also has some disadvantages regarding economic and technical issues in SCM. Because

RFID technology needs massive investment and the return on investment is longer, it has a risk of obsolescence and a high level of innovation. Increasingly implemented in the apparel industry for some years, RFID technology has become mature and has a long future.

References

ABI Research (2009). *RFID Item-Level Tagging in Fashion Apparel and Footwear*. Available at: www.abiresearch.com/market-research/product/1006979-rfid-item-level-tagging-in-fashion-and-app/.

Adaptalift (2012). *RFID vs Barcodes: Advantages and disadvantages comparison*. Available at: www.aalhysterforklifts.com.au/index.php/about/blogpost/rfid_vs_barcodes_advantages_and_disadvantages_comparison.

Attaran, M. (2012). *Critical Success Factors and Challenges of Implementing RFID in Supply Chain Management* [online]. Available at: http://csupom.org/PUBLICATIONS/2012-1/JSCOM_2012-1-11.pdf.

Automatic I.D. News Asia (1998a). Alto Group hits high notes with new inventory management system March/April, pp. 26–28.

Automatic I.D. News Asia (1998b). RF cuts processing time for Lexus car and parts deliveries, August/September [online], pp. 30–34.

Azevedo, S.G. & Carvalho, H. (2012). Contribution of RFID technology to better management of fashion supply chains. *International Journal of Retail & Distribution Management*, 40(2), pp. 128–156.

Balocco, R., Miragliotta, G., Perego, A. & Tumino, A. (2011). RFID adoption in the FMCG supply chain: An interpretative framework [online], *Supply Chain Management: An International Journal*, 16(5), pp. 299–315. Available at: http://dx.doi.org/10.1108/13598541111155820.

Bjork, Christopher (2014). ZARA builds its business around RFID. *Wall Street Journal*, Available at: www.wsj.com/articles/at-zara-fast-fashion-meets-smarter-inventory-1410884519.

Blecker, T. & Huang, G.Q. (2008). *RFID in Operations and Supply Chain Management*. Erich Schmidt Verlag, p. 258. Available at: books.google.co.uk/books?id=IBgrYdD_y8cC&pg=PA258&lpg=PA258&dq=storage+capacity+RFID+tag+and+barcodes&source=bl&ots=TXrx3VMsd6&sig=f3cz4PuknF6P1UlppPlVAUP-8PQ&hl=en&sa=X&ei=Kuc3VavbKYvcaO-HgPAB&ved=0CFIQ6AEwCA#v=onepage&q&f=false.

Bogan, C. & Callahan, D. (2001). Benchmarking in rapid time. *Industrial Management*, 43(2), pp. 28–33.

Charikleia, L. (2010). *RFID in the Retailing Supply Chain: A Case Study on a Fashion Retailing Industry* [online]. Available at: https://gupea.ub.gu.se/bitstream/2077/22606/1/gupea_2077_22606_1.pdf.

Chopra, S. & Meindl, P. (2013). *Supply Chain Management Strategy, Planning, and Operation: What is a supply chain*, 5th edn. London: Pearson Education.

Collins, J. (2005). Marks & Spencer to Extend Trial to 53 Stores. *RFID Journal* [online]. Available at: www.rfidjournal.com/articles/view?1412.

Cronin, R. (2009). What is the Future of RFID? *Intermec, Field Technology* [online]. Available at: www.fieldtechnologiesonline.com/doc/what-is-the-future-of-rfid-0001.

Grieco, P.T. et al. (1989). *Behind Bars: Bar coding principles and applications*. PT Publications.

GS1 Memove (2012). Case Study: Inventory Management in Apparel [online]. Available at: www.gs1.org/sites/default/files/2012_05_gs1brazil_memove.pdf.

Guercini, S. (n.d.). *Traceability along the supply chain and its impact on buyer-seller relationships: Evidences from the fashion industry* [online]. Available at: http://libra.msra.cn/Publication/6976312/traceability-along-the-supply-chain-and-its-impact-on-buyer-seller-relationships-evidences-from-the.

Hellström, D. & Wiberg, M. (2010). Improving inventory accuracy using RFID technology: A case study. *Assembly Automation*, 30(4), pp. 345–351.

Herand, D. (2014). QR Code Usage for Marketing Activities of Logistics Companies. *Management*, 4(3A), pp. 27–33 [online]. Available at: http://article.sapub.org/10.5923.s.mm.201401.04.html [accessed 13 March 2015].

Inditex (2014). *Radio frequency identification (RFID) project* [online]. Available at: www.inditex.com/media/news_article?articleId=150174.

Kwok, S.K. & Wu, K.K.W. (2009). RFID-based intra-supply chain in textile industry. *Industrial Management & Data Systems*, 109(9), pp. 1166–1178. Available at: http://dx.doi.org/10.1108/02635570911002252.

Lambert, S. (2011). Adidas replaces recruiters with QR codes. *Mobile Commerce News*. Available at: www.qrcodepress.com/adidas-replaces-recruiters-with-qr-codes/855410/.

McCathie, L. (2004). *The advantages and disadvantages of barcodes and radio frequency identification in supply chain management*. University of Wollongong. Available at: http://ro.uow.edu.au/cgi/viewcontent.cgi?article=1009&context=thesesinfo.

Meyers, R. (2000). The ten commandments of bar coding. *Frontline Solutions* (August), pp. A5–A22.

Moon, K.L. & Ngai, E.W.T. (2008). The adoption of RFID in fashion retailing: A business value-added framework. *Industrial Management & Data Systems*, 108(5), pp. 596–612 [online]. Available at: http://dx.doi.org/10.1108/02635570810876732.

Palmer, R.C. (1995). *The Bar Code Book: Reading, Printing and Specification of Bar Code Symbols*. New Hampshire: Helmers Publishing Inc.

Roberti, M. (2013). Bloomingdale's and Others Say RFID Works. *RFID Journal* [online]. Available at: www.rfidjournal.com/articles/view?10673.

Russell, E. (2010). Key factors to consider in choosing the correct data collection technology for your customer. *The Media Journal* [online]. Available at: www.themhedajournal.org/2010/07/12/bar-codes-or-rfid-tags/.

Seideman, T. (2011). *Barcodes Sweep the World, Barcode Incorporated* [online]. Available at: www.barcoding.com/information/barcode_history.shtml.

Simon, Serge (2011). *Les codes-barres et les puces RFID que choisir? Infos pour les pros de la vente, logistique et industrie* [online]. Available at: www.professionnels.eu/archives/364.

Supply Chain Digest (2013). JC Penney's Sudden Retreat from RFID Led to Rash of Store Thefts. Available at: www.scdigest.com/ontarget/13-12-03-1.php?cid=7637.

Wamba, S. Fosso (2012). Achieving supply chain integration using RFID technology: The case of emerging intelligent B-to-B ecommerce processes in a living laboratory. *Business Process Management Journal*, 18(1), pp. 58–81 [online]. Available at: www.researchgate.net/profile/Samuel_Fosso_Wamba/publication/235283479_Achieving_supply_chain_integration_using_RFID_technology_The_case_of_emerging_intelligent_B-to-B_e-commerce_processes_in_a_living_laboratory/links/0deec533481a1759bf000000.pdf.

Zetes (2009). *(R)evolution of the Market for Voice Solutions in Europe: A White Paper*. Available at: www.retail-systems.com/rs/whitepapers/WP_%28r%29evolution_of_the_market_for_voice.pdf [accessed 12 February 2018].

6

CONSUMER BEHAVIOUR AND THE FASHION SUPPLY CHAIN

Klassen and Vachon (2006) state that the manager of a supply chain must explicitly recognise linkages to related disciplines, and broaden the theoretical framework by the integration of theories from closely related fields of research. There are overlaps between marketing and supply chain management functions, such as services (Jüttner et al., 2010). The coordination of marketing and supply chain departments often results in improved customer service-related performance (Ellinger et al., 2000). Supply chain management models such as lean management (Christopher, 2000; Mo, 2015), agile management (Yusuf et al., 1999; Routroy & Shankar, 2015), and demand chain management (Park et al., 2015) have been improving company efficiency and their ability to respond to consumer demand.

Quality management has evolved into new topics of research such as lean and consumer management (Cudney & Elrod, 2010). Consumer awareness and demand for new products and services will also accelerate the adoption of new practices. It is obvious that consumer behaviour has a direct causal relation with the performance of the whole supply chain. This chapter will discuss in detail consumer behaviour in fashion.

6.1 Consumer purchasing behaviour

Consumer purchasing behaviour can be considered as a course of events in which people search for, choose and buy merchandise in order to create the satisfaction of their demand and longing (Belch & Belch, 2004). Churchill and Peter (1998) stated that there are three main factors affecting the consumer purchasing process: social factors, situational factors, and marketing factors. Social effects include the social class of the consumer, the influence of family and education, culture and subculture. Also consumers' actions, impressions and feelings are affected by their reference group. Consumers are always influenced by the moments they have experienced. Such influence can be divided into situational factors. According to Park, Iyer and Smith (1989), the social environment, physical circumstances, people's temporary emotions, time and financial conditions are the major elements of situational influences. Churchill and Peter (1998) stated that the social surroundings include people's interactions, consumer traits and duty. Also consumers' mood states, time available and money conditions will affect their purchasing decision at the moment when the purchase happens. And the physical circumstances involve the display and layout of the store, the internal and external design of the store, the position of the store and the degree of noise in the store. Marketing factors influence consumer purchasing behaviour in many aspects. Marketing effects involve the marketing mix, information about products, price, location and promotion.

6.2 Impulse purchasing behaviour

As part of consumer behaviour, impulse purchasing behaviour differs significantly from other shopping behaviours in many aspects. The definition of impulse purchasing was first created by DuPont studies in 1948. According to earlier literature, impulse purchasing behaviour was defined to be the same as unplanned purchasing behaviour (Applebaum, 1951; Bellenger et al.. 1978). Stern (1962) stated that impulse purchasing is a substitute for unplanned purchasing. This definition of impulse purchasing behaviour was affirmed by many scholars at that time (Cobb & Hoyer, 1986; Kollat & Willett, 1967). Norman and Bobrow (1975) defined impulse purchasing as any purchases not written on someone's shopping list. Weinberg and Gottwald (1982) defined impulse purchasing behaviour as a thoughtless action and a rapid action. And they also considered impulse buying behaviour is a notion which covers decision making. But it is neither regular nor rational. They stated that although all impulse purchasing is unplanned, not all unplanned purchasing is done impulsively. Bellenger, Robertson and Hirschman (1978) considered that impulse purchasing could best be defined in terms of whether the purchaser made the decision to purchase prior to or after entering the store. Based on Rook's (1987) statement, impulse purchases are a sudden and powerful urge which enable people to purchase things immediately. Piron (1991) stated that impulse purchasing behaviour has four main characteristics: it is an unplanned purchase, the consequence of exposure to a stimulus, the response to affection or cognition, and is determined 'on the spot'.

Baumeister, Heatherton and Tice (1994) defined that impulse purchasing behaviour is not a potential or ordinary trait and lust, but is a specific desire or motivation to accomplish a special action. Beatty and Ferrell (1998) extended the previous definition of impulse purchasing as an abrupt and unexpected purchasing behaviour without any pre-shopping intentions. And it did not need to finish the purchasing tasks and buy products from a specific item category. This behaviour is instinctive and spontaneous, and it happened after the experience of the shopping urge.

After 2000, there appeared many later definitions of impulse purchasing behaviour. Pooler (2003) considered that impulse purchasing is a no-plan action to purchase the object. An impulse purchasing decision needs to be made in an extremely short time; the consumer made the purchase decision in a situation in which they did not obtain comprehensive product information (Jones et al., 2003). Gutierrez (2004) stated impulse purchasing as the behaviour when consumers buy items in a particular situation: consumers are not clear about what they want and whether it is in their budget. And consumers will also ignore the consequences of post-purchase. Sharma et al. (2010) defined impulse buying as sudden, complex purchase behaviour. When people are shopping on impulse, they always make decisions rapidly and consider them incomplete. According to various literature, the definition of impulse purchasing behaviour has changed in every period, and the definition of impulse purchasing has evolved over the past 50 years.

6.2.1 The features of impulse purchasing

Rook and Hoch (1985) thought there are five characteristics that help people to distinguish impulsive from non-impulsive consumer behaviour.

Firstly, impulse purchasing behaviour is different from the usual purchasing behaviour. It lets consumers have an abrupt and instinctive desire. After that, consumers will undertake the purchasing behaviour impulsively. This is a concept that mental status changes rapidly.

The second feature of impulse purchasing is to solve the psychological problem of consumer. A consumer can resolve the mental imbalance through an abrupt urge to buy. This characteristic of impulse purchasing may let people have a feeling of temporary lack of control.

Thirdly, impulse purchasing behaviour may cause mental struggle or mental conflict (Thaler & Shefrin, 1981). When consumers do the impulse purchasing, they will have an ambivalent feeling to the object merchandise. Consumers need to measure the value of goods and the consequences of this impulse buying behaviour immediately, so they will have a strong psychological struggle. In many cases, people conduct impulse buying behaviour because it enables them to obtain satisfaction immediately.

The fourth feature of impulse purchasing behaviour is the change in people's cognitive evaluation. When customers purchase on impulse, most of them will pay less attention to the cognitive assessment of the merchandise. According to Weinberg and Gottwald (1982), typical transrational and emotional states are features of impulse purchases. Impulse buying behaviour will increase the emotional activation of the consumer. This led people to feel the behaviour of impulse is 'automatic' and out of control. The urge created from impulse purchasing behaviour can widely alter consumers' attention points, making consumers change the original purchasing process.

The last characteristic of impulse purchasing behaviour is lack of consideration of the consequences. When consumers buy something impulsively, they often do so without considering the result of this behaviour. According to Kipnis (1971), impulsiveness has the ability to transform an individual's personality and decision

68 Consumer behaviour in fashion

making. Similarly to Wishnie's (1977) statement, people in an impulse status when purchasing will focus more on their current feelings, and pay less attention to the future consequences after the impulse purchasing behaviour.

6.2.2 Categories of impulse purchasing

Based on Cobb and Hoyer's (1986) statement, consumer impulse purchasing behaviour can be divided into three kinds, namely planner, partial planner and impulse purchaser. The classification of these three categories is according to consumers' intent of purchasing from a certain merchandise category or a brand.

Although Cobb and Hoyer's classification of impulse purchasing is inclusive, it is still too broad and not specific enough. Nevertheless, Stern (1962) offered a more comprehensive classification of impulse purchasing behaviour, namely pure impulse purchasing, reminder impulse purchasing, suggestion impulse purchasing and planned impulse purchasing.

Pure impulse purchasing is the easiest to be differentiated from the other kinds of impulse purchasing behaviour, although it may occupy a relatively small proportion among all impulse purchases. It is unique and it demolishes the normal purchasing patterns. This kind of purchasing does not need any idea or plan before buying (Han et al., 1991). Compared with ordinary purchasing behaviour, pure impulse purchasing is a really simple purchasing behaviour which depends on impulse stimulation. And pure impulse purchasing is generated by affective appeal (McGoldrick, 2002; Jeffrey & Hodge, 2007). For instance, when someone is waiting in the queue for checkout, a magazine catches his eye, and he is attracted by the images on the cover of the magazine. In this example, the consumer generated the desire and an urge to purchase the magazine due to the affective appeal, so this is typical pure impulse purchasing behaviour.

Compared with Churchill and Peter's (1998) consumer purchasing process model, the impulse purchasing process model created by Kim (2003) looks more simple. Because impulse purchasing behaviour omitted a few steps on the basis of general consumer purchasing behaviour, like 'need recognition', 'information search' and 'alternative evaluation'. He also reclassified the factors that affect this purchasing behaviour. The first step of the impulse purchasing process is product awareness. Impulse consumers start to browse a certain commodity or enter a shop without any purchase intention.

According to Verplanken et al. (2005), impulse purchasing's fundamental function is to reduce negative emotions. A similar statement considered that people's usual impulse purchasing behaviour is an expression of escaping negative feelings and self-humiliation. Moreover, Vojvodic and Matic (2014) stated that one of the functions of impulse purchasing is to release emotions such as happiness, anxiety, applause, joy and envy.

Hausman (2000) considered that hedonism is the main motivation of impulse purchasing. Consumers want to obtain surprise, newness and change through impulse purchases (Holbrook & Hirschman, 1982; Hirschman, 1980). Similar reports from customers show that impulse purchasing can meet their need for hedonic demands (Piron, 1991; Rook, 1987; Thompson et al., 1990).

6.3 Product characteristics

Rook and Hoch (1985) found that the product is a major factor which influences consumer impulse purchasing behaviour. Based on the studies from marketing research, all the items can be classified in two categories, which are functional items and hedonistic items. Babin et al. (1994) stated that customers bought hedonic products primarily for the purpose of enjoyment, but purchases of functional products create utilitarian values. Investigation showed that more consumer impulse purchasing behaviour happened in hedonic products, because hedonic products are a symbol of hedonism and can convey a sense of pleasure.

According to trade journals, products with brighter colours, gifts and specific premiums can trigger the urge for consumer impulse purchases. However, almost everything can be bought impulsively. Some products like electronic devices, books and expensive outfits may be regarded as non-impulse items, but their purchase may implicate impulsive behaviour. Rook and Hoch (1985) considered that consumer impulse purchasing is widespread, which goes beyond the boundaries of product categories and the population. Bellenger, Robertson and Hirschman (1978) indicated that about 40% of consumers' consumption in department stores can be classified in the impulse category. Each product line has about 27% to 62% of total sales due to impulse buying; only limited product lines are not influenced by impulse purchasing.

Furthermore, McGoldrick (2002) also indicated that the extent of consumer impulse purchasing depends on the different types of product. For example, a study stated that more than 60% of consumers' jewellery consumption was unplanned in emporiums. However, over the past 50 years' studies, the category of impulse purchase products has been inconsistent. And it is hard for researchers to define which products are most likely to trigger impulse purchasing, but generally, impulse purchases can be influenced by the product with two properties and characteristics: 'product line' and 'price'. Moreover, it is proven that consumers frequently have bought the product with smaller size, lighter weight and easier storage on impulse.

Kotler (1991) stated that plentiful advertising may create the occurrence of consumer impulse purchasing behaviour. Because advertising lets consumers create the knowledge about the brand or the product, this increases the possibility that the consumer will identify the item and purchase the item impulsively. Mass advertisements make a huge contribution to this target directly, because it lets consumers know more product information, function and detail. In addition, Stern (1962) found that plenty of impulse purchasing, especially planned impulse purchasing and reminder impulse purchasing, depend on the level of consumer cognition of the product. This knowledge is formed by consumers' previous shopping experience, the evaluation and recommendation of other people, and from mass advertisements. Although the major purpose of plentiful advertising is to form customers' planned purchases of a specific product or brand in advance, the reminder from mass advertising causes the occurrence of impulse purchasing to a large extent.

70 Consumer behaviour in fashion

6.4 Consumer characteristics

Except for factors like store, product and promotion, consumers themselves own a variety of characteristics which can influence impulse purchasing behaviour. Consumer characteristics can be divided into personal factors and environmental factors which happened at the time of purchase.

Wood (2005) noted that age is an influential factor to consumer impulse purchasing behaviour. Similarly, Kacen and Lee (2002) found that consumer impulse purchase tendencies are associated with some demographic features like an individual's age. When shopping, young people always receive fewer risks, they tend to spend more money on various products they want. Compared with younger people, older people may be more rational when spending money. People aged from 18 to 39 are the age group in which impulse purchases most occurred. Similar findings was found by Bellenger et al. (1978), who noted that compared with consumers more than 35 years old, consumers under 35 are more likely to purchase on impulse. Moreover, studies of trait impulsiveness found that the score of younger people in impulsivity measure is higher than the score of older people (Eysenck et al., 1985; Helmers et al., 1995; Rawling et al., 1995). This also proves that young people's self-control is not as good as that of adults (Logue & Chavarro, 1992).

Kacen and Lee (2002) stated that gender is a demographic factor which influences consumer impulse purchasing behaviour. In addition, Dittmar et al. (1995) found that females are more likely to do impulse purchasing than males. Researchers noted that women tend to pay more attention to values of relationship-oriented and affective, but men tend to pay more attention to values of implemental and functional. The study also showed that males focus on personal agreement in purchasing while females focus more on social agreement. That is the reason why women always do impulse purchase.

Kacen and Lee (2002) found that culture is an influential factor to consumer impulse purchasing behaviour in both individual aspect and regional aspect. Culture can be divided into individualist culture and collectivist culture. Podoshen and Andrzejewski (2012) stated that impulse purchasing is correlated with fastuous consumption and materialism. Moreover, Richins and Dawson (1992) noted that materialistic people always purchase product impulsively as the pattern of self-completion. According to Tatzel (2002), materialistic people are always less strict in managing their money, they always present a positive viewpoint toward impulse purchasing behaviour. Based on Watson's (2003) study, people with high materialistic value tend to spend more money on purchases. And Belk (1995) considered that materialistic people may even indulge in impulse shopping.

McGoldrick (2002) found that shopping enjoyment may lead to impulse purchasing by delivering several hedonic values to consumers. Similarly, Beatty and Ferrell (1998) noted that people regard shopping as a kind of reaction, and it is not directly linked to their purchasing list. Therefore, they will browse longer and this often results in more purchases on impulse. Similarly, Bellenger and Korgaonkar (1980) defined recreational shoppers as the people who relished shopping. And recreational shoppers are likely to spend more time browsing in the store and make purchase decisions on impulse.

Beatty and Ferrell (1998) found that there is a direct link between impulse purchasing tendency and impulse purchasing behaviour. Rook (1987) noted that an impulse purchasing tendency determines the propensity of a person to purchase on impulse. Based on research, consumers who have a higher score in impulse buying tendency tend to experience more impulsive urges and purchase more impulsively when shopping (Beatty & Ferrell, 1998).

Beatty and Ferrell (1998) noted that consumers' available time for shopping decided whether they would purchase on impulse. A consumer who has extra available time tends to browse longer in shopping surroundings, increasing the possibility of purchasing on impulse. On the other hand, shopping in a hurry reduces browsing time, which means fewer products would be browsed with less possibility of purchase on impulse (Silvera et al., 2008). Moreover, Iyer (1989) indicated that time pressure (limited time to shop) tended to decrease the occurrence of impulse purchasing.

Beatty and Ferrell (1998) found that the amount of available money is an influential factor which encourages impulse purchasing behaviour. Financial availability directly improves purchasing power. In a shopping environment, people tend to avoid purchasing behaviour if they do not have adequate money. Furthermore, Silvera et al. (2008) noted that available money is the prime mover in the impulse purchasing process. Similarly, Jeon (1990) stated that the availability of funds directly interrelated with impulse buying, and it is the facilitator for buying the desired item.

References

Applebaum, W. (1951). Studying customer behavior in retail stores. *The Journal of Marketing*, pp.172–178.

Babin, B.J., Darden, W.R. & Griffin, L.A. (1994). Negative emotions in marketing research: Affect or artifact? *Journal of Business Research*, 42(3), pp. 271–285.

Baumeister, R.F., Heatherton, T.F. & Tice, D.M. (1994). *Losing Control: How and Why People Fail at Self-regulation*. Academic Press.

Beatty, S.E. & Ferrell, M.E. (1998). Impulse buying: Modeling its precursors. *Journal of Retailing*, 74(2), pp. 169–191.

Belch, G. & Belch, M. (2004). *Advertising and Promotion: An Integrated Marketing Communications Perspective*, 6th edn. New York: McGraw-Hill.

Belk, R.W. (1995). Collecting as luxury consumption: Effects on individuals and households. *Journal of Economic Psychology*, 16(3), pp. 477–490.

Bellenger, D.N. & Korgaonkar, P.K. (1980). Profiling the recreational shopper. *Journal of Retailing*, 56(3), pp. 77–92.

Bellenger, D.N., Robertson, D.H. & Hirschman, E.C. (1978). Impulse buying varies by product. *Journal of Advertising Research*, 18(6), pp. 15–18.

Christopher, M. (2000). The Agile Supply Chain: Competing in Volatile Markets. *Industrial Marketing Management*, 29(1), pp. 37–44.

Churchill, G.A. & Peter, J.P. (1998). *Marketing: Creating Value for Customers*. Irwin/McGraw Hill.

Cobb, C.J. & Hoyer, W.D. (1986). Planned versus impulse purchase behavior. *Journal of Retailing*.

Cudney, E. & Elrod, C. (2010). Incorporating lean concepts into supply chain management. *International Journal of Six Sigma and Competitive Advantage*, 6(1–2), pp. 12–30.

Dawson, S. & Kim, M. (2010). Cues on apparel web sites that trigger impulse purchases. *Journal of Fashion Marketing and Management: An International Journal*, 14(2), pp. 230–246.

Dittmar, H., Beattie, J. & Friese, S. (1995). Gender identity and material symbols: Objects and decision considerations in impulse purchases. *Journal of Economic Psychology*, 16(3), pp. 491–511.

Ellinger, A.E., Daugherty, P.J. & Keller, S.B. (2000). The relationship between marketing/logistics interdepartmental integration and performance in U.S. manufacturing firms: An empirical study. *Journal of Business Logistics*, 21(1), pp. 1–22.

Eysenck, S.B., Pearson, P.R., Easting, G. & Allsopp, J.F. (1985). Age norms for impulsiveness, venturesomeness and empathy in adults. *Personality and Individual Differences*, 6(5), pp. 613–619.

Gutierrez, B.P.B. (2004). Determinants of planned and impulse buying: The case of the Philippines. *Asia Pacific Management Review*, 9(6), pp. 1061–1078.

Han, Y.K., Morgan, G.A., Kotsiopulos, A. & Kang-Park, J. (1991). Impulse buying behavior of apparel purchasers. *Clothing and Textiles Research Journal*, 9(3), pp. 15–21.

Hausman, A. (2000). A multi-method investigation of consumer motivations in impulse buying behavior. *Journal of Consumer Marketing*, 17(5), pp. 403–426.

Helmers, K.F., Young, S.N. & Pihl, R. (1995). Assessment of measures of impulsivity in healthy male volunteers. *Personality and Individual Differences*, 19, pp. 927–935.

Hirschman, E.C. (1980). Innovativeness, novelty seeking, and consumer creativity. *Journal of Consumer Research*, pp. 283–295.

Holbrook, M.B. & Hirschman, E.C. (1982). The experiential aspects of consumption: Consumer fantasies, feelings, and fun. *Journal of Consumer Research*, pp. 132–140.

Iyer, E.S. (1989). Unplanned purchasing: Knowledge of shopping environment and time pressure. *Journal of Retailing*, 65(1), pp. 40–58.

Jeffrey, S.A. & Hodge, R. (2007). Factors influencing impulse buying during an online purchase. *Electronic Commerce Research*, 7(3–4), pp. 367–379.

Jeon, J.O. (1990). *An empirical investigation of the relationship between affective states, in-store browsing, and impulse buying*. Thesis, University of Alabama.

Jones, M.A., Reynolds, K.E., Weun, S. & Beatty, S.E. (2003). The product-specific nature of impulse buying tendency. *Journal of Business Research*, 56(7), pp. 505–511.

Jüttner, U., Martin, C. & Godsell, J. (2010). A strategic framework for integrating marketing and supply chain strategies. *International Journal of Logistics Management*, 21(1), pp. 104–126.

Kacen, J.J. & Lee, J.A. (2002). The influence of culture on consumer impulsive buying behavior. *Journal of Consumer Psychology*, 12(2), pp. 163–176.

Kim, J. (2003). *College students' apparel impulse buying behaviors in relation to visual merchandising*. Los Angeles: American Intercontinental University.

Kipnis, D. (1971). *Character Structure and Impulsiveness*, Vol. 9. Academic Press.

Klassen, R.D. & Vachon, S. (2006). Extending Green Practices Across the Supply Chain. The Impact of Upstream and Downstream Integration. *International Journal of Operations & Production Management*, 26(7), pp. 795–821.

Kollat, D.T. & Willett, R.P. (1967). Customer impulse purchasing behavior. *Journal of Marketing Research*, pp. 21–31.

Kotler, P. (1991). *Marketing Management*, 7th edn. New Jersey: Prentice-Hall.

Logue, A.W. & Chavarro, A. (1992). Self-control and impulsiveness in preschool children. *Psychological Record*, 42, pp. 189–203.

McGoldrick, P. (2002). *Retail Marketing*, 2nd edn. London: McGraw-Hill Education.

Mo, Z. (2015). Internationalization Process of Fast Fashion Retailers: Evidence of H&M and Zara. *International Journal of Business and Management*, 10(3), pp. 217–236.

Norman, D.A. & Bobrow, D.G. (1975). On data-limited and resource-limited processes. *Cognitive Psychology*, 7(1), pp. 44–64.

Park, C.W., Iyer, E.S. & Smith, D.C. (1989). The effects of situational factors on in-store grocery shopping behavior: The role of store environment and time available for shopping. *Journal of Consumer Research*, pp. 422–433.

Park, Y.W., Shintaku, J. & Hong, P. (2015). Effective supply chain integration: Case studies for Korean global firms in China. *International Journal of Manufacturing Technology and Management*, 29(3–4), p. 161.

Piron, F. (1991). Defining Impulse Purchasing. *Advances in Consumer Research*, 18, pp. 509–514.

Podoshen, J.S. & Andrzejewski, S.A. (2012). An examination of the relationships between materialism, conspicuous consumption, impulse buying, and brand loyalty. *Journal of Marketing Theory and Practice*, 20(3), pp. 319–334.

Pooler, J.A. (2003). *Why we shop: Emotional rewards and retail strategies*. Greenwood Publishing Group.

Rawling, D., Boldero, J. & Wiseman, F. (1995). The interaction of age with impulsiveness and venturesomeness in the prediction of adolescent sexual behavior. *Personality and Individual Differences*, 19(1), pp. 117–120.

Richins, M.L. & Dawson, S. (1992). A consumer values orientation for materialism and its measurement: Scale development and validation. *Journal of Consumer Research*, 19, December, pp. 303–316.

Rook, D.W. (1987). The buying impulse. *Journal of Consumer Research*, pp. 189–199.

Rook, D.W. & Hoch, S.J. (1985). Consuming impulses. *Advances in Consumer Research*, 12 (1), pp. 23–27.

Routroy, S. & Shankar, A. (2015). Performance analysis of agile supply chain. *International Journal of Manufacturing Technology and Management*, 29(3–4), p. 180.

Sharma, P., Sivakumaran, B. & Marshall, R. (2010). Impulse buying and variety seeking: A trait-correlates perspective. *Journal of Business Research*, 63(3), pp. 276–283.

Silvera, D.H., Lavack, A.M. & Kropp, F. (2008). Impulse buying: The role of affect, social influence, and subjective wellbeing. *Journal of Consumer Marketing*, 25(1), pp. 23–33.

Stern, H. (1962). The significance of impulse buying today. *The Journal of Marketing*, pp. 59–62.

Tatzel, M. (2002). 'Money worlds' and well-being: An integration of money dispositions, materialism and price-related behavior. *Journal of Economic Psychology*, 23(1), pp. 103–126.

Thaler, R.H. & Shefrin, H.M. (1981). An economic theory of self-control. *Journal of Political Economy*, 89, pp. 392–406.

Thompson, C.J., Locander, W.B. & Pollio, H.R. (1990). The lived meaning of free choice: An existential-phenomenological description of everyday consumer experiences of contemporary married women. *Journal of Consumer Research*, pp. 346–361.

Verplanken, B., Herabadi, A.G., Perry, J.A. & Silvera, D.H. (2005). Consumer style and health: The role of impulsive buying in unhealthy eating. *Psychology and Health*, 20(4), pp. 429–441.

Vojvodic, K. & Matic, M. (2014). Challenges of e-Retailing: Impulsive Buying Behaviour. *International Business and Management*, 29, pp. 155–171.

Watson, J.J. (2003). The relationship of materialism to spending tendencies, saving, and debt. *Journal of Economic Psychology*, 24(6), pp. 723–739.

Weinberg, P. & Gottwald, W. (1982). Impulsive consumer buying as a result of emotions. *Journal of Business Research*, 10(1), pp. 43–57.

Wishnie, H.A. (1977). *The impulsive personality*. Springer Science and Business Media.

Wood, M. (2005). Discretionary unplanned buying in consumer society. *Journal of Consumer Behaviour*, 4(4), pp. 268–281.

Yusuf, Y.Y., Sarhadi, M. & Gunasekaran, A. (1999). Agile manufacturing: The drivers, concepts and attributes. *International Journal of Production Economics*, 62(1–2), pp. 33–43.

7

RESEARCH METHODOLOGIES FOR FASHION SUPPLY CHAIN ANALYSIS

The main purpose of this chapter is to discuss different research and analysis methods which are suitable for fashion supply chain management.

7.1 Introduction

Ellram (1996) argues that logistics research may benefit from the use of case studies as a methodology. Mentzer and Flint (1997), and Garver and Mentzer (1999) claimed that analysed supply chain dimensions need vigorous analytical validation such as structural equation modelling.

Voss et al. (2002) provided a comprehensive guideline for approaching case studies in operations management. Gammelgaard (1997) describes how the evolution of a joint PhD programme in logistics includes 'methods in logistics research'. Näslund (2002) identified the use of the action approach for research design in logistics.

Research methods 'refer to the techniques and procedures used to obtain and analyse data', while research methodology 'refers to the theory of how research should be undertaken' (Saunders et al., 2007, p.387). Easterby-Smith et al. (2008) believe the examination of research philosophy is essential for researchers to evaluate, refine and specify the methodologies to lead to appropriate use of research methods and strategies. Therefore, it is important to start this chapter with an overview of research philosophy and consider a number of philosophical assumptions and their implications for the method or methods used. This is followed by discussions on research approach, data collection and analysis methods including research design, validity and reliability of the study.

7.2 Research philosophy

Research philosophy is the attitude held by researchers towards the method in which data are gathered, analysed and applied, and is determined by the way in which one views the world and the assumptions associated with such views (Saunders et al., 2007). The way one views the world is described by the ontology (the nature of reality), and epistemology (the knowledge of the reality), which together shape the research strategies and methods (Saunders et al., 2007). Earlier researchers such as Seaker et al. (1993) discussed the need for more formal contributions of research to theory. Arlbjørn and Halldórsson (2002), and Mentzer and Kahn (1995) stated that research methodology is important in generating supply chain knowledge, theory and practice.

7.2.1 Ontology

Ontology is 'the study of being and involves ideas related to human existence, the nature of being and social reality' (Daymon & Holloway, 2011, p.100). There are three categories of ontology: objectivism, subjectivism and constructivism. Dietz (2006) defined them as follows: Objectivism portrays the view that an environment including the world, exists entirely independent from social actors and therefore reality is taken as given. Subjectivism describes the completely/complete opposite view that perceptions of the world are created by the social actors themselves and therefore the image of reality holds a different meaning in the eye of the subject where no one can interpret for others (Jones et al., 2006). Constructivism stands between objectivism and subjectivism and states that all knowledge and reality is gained through the experiences of social actors and the interactions between human beings and the world, which is continuously adapting (Crotty, 1998).

7.2.2 Epistemology

Epistemology is 'the philosophical study or theory of knowledge and determines what counts for valid knowledge' (Daymon & Holloway, 2011, p.100). Epistemology provides credibility in knowledge and a framework to create reproducible results using rigorous methodology. There are various views and assumptions regarding epistemology due to the different beliefs surrounding ontology and subsections of epistemology. Under the study of epistemology, there are a number of philosophies, and some commonly adapted philosophies in practical research are positivism, realism and interpretivism (Easterby-Smith et al., 2008).

7.2.3 Positivism

Positivism holds the ontological belief of objectivism and believes 'the world is external to the researcher and is something "out there" waiting to be discovered, with the research's "discovery" of that reality directly reflecting it' (Daymon &

Holloway, 2011, p.101). The aim of a positivist's research is to seek rules and patterns of the world to explain social behaviour using a scientific approach where the social reality is observable. Due to the positivist's beliefs of knowledge and reality, positivists usually apply quantitative methods and one is void of value in the research.

7.2.4 Interpretivism

Interpretivism holds the ontological belief of subjectivism and requires an empathetic stance, looking at a situation from the point of view of the social actors to gain understanding rather than scientific explanation (Bryman, 2007). Interpretivists are opposed to the generalised, rule-driven methods of the positivist, and believe the relationship between reality and the mind of social actors is essential to understand in order to conduct valuable research. Therefore, interpretivists usually apply qualitative methods to gain in-depth descriptions of attitudes, feelings and values of individuals or small groups of individuals (Bryman, 2007).

7.2.5 Realism

Realism combines the fundamentals from both positivism and interpretivism. 'The essence of realism is that what the senses show us as reality is the truth: that objects have an existence independent of the human mind' (Easterby-Smith et al., 1997). Realism stands by a belief that reality exists independent of human consciousness and defines knowledge as being entirely socially invented, where our perception of the real world is a socially pressurised outcome (Saunders et al., 2007). However, Marsh and Furlong (2002, p.30) argued that 'not all social phenomena, and the relationships between them, are directly observable. There are deep structures that cannot be observed and what can be observed may offer a false picture of those phenomena/structures and their effects'. Therefore, a realist believes that reality can exist on multiple levels (Chia, 2002), and thus research can be undertaken at different levels and from different points of view, all combining into a common goal.

7.2.6 Pragmatism

'Pragmatism argues that the most important determinant of the epistemology, ontology and axiology you adopt is the research question – one may be more appropriate than the other for answering particular questions' (Saunders et al., 2009, p.109). When the adapted philosophy is unclear, it is more than likely the researcher is a pragmatist who believes it is possible to have variations in epistemology, ontology and axiology. Tashakkori and Teddlie (1998) suggest it is important that a researcher sees research philosophy as being in a continuum instead of being at two extremes. Pragmatism allows researchers to focus on selecting the most suitable methods in answering the research question instead of questioning about the truth and reality; however, it has been argued that

78 Research methodologies

pragmatism creates smaller and less revolutionary changes to a situation or problem than more extreme methods (Saunders et al., 2009), and agreed by Johnson and Onwuegbuzie (2004), who believe pragmatism is often rather vague in its findings, making it difficult to determine usefulness unless the researcher specifically agrees on a 'good' result. Pragmatism is also supported by Guba and Lincoln (1994, p.105), who stated, 'both qualitative and quantitative methods may be used appropriately with any research paradigm. Questions of method are secondary to questions of paradigm, which we define as the basic belief system or world view that guides the investigation, not only in choices of method but in ontologically and epistemologically fundamental ways'. This research holds the view of a pragmatist.

7.3 Research approach

The research approach focuses on systematic ways of looking at a problem and it supports the framing of research design. There are mainly two types of research approach in developing theory – inductive and deductive – and some researchers use both approaches in the same piece of research (Saunders et al., 2007). A deductive approach focuses on testing a theory while an inductive approach focuses on generating a theory. The types of research approach used can be viewed in terms of research philosophy. Positivists often apply a deductive approach while an interpretivist is more likely to apply an inductive approach; however, there is no valid practical value to label as such, as it can be misleading (Saunders et al., 2007).

A deductive approach uses theory to establish a hypothesis for testing in order to either accept or reject the hypothesis (Trochim, 2006). To test the hypothesis, quantitative data are usually collected and the researcher is independent of the observation. This method of research is most often used in the natural sciences where a large amount of literature on the subject is available, making the construction of a sensible hypothesis relatively straightforward. Once a hypothesis is established, a rigorous, structured method is set to allow efficient data collection and analysis to confirm the hypothesis. Such methods require a large amount of data collection in order to allow for the generalisation of hypothesis and results.

An inductive approach allows new, under-researched topics to be studied (Trochim, 2006). New topics with very little existing literature may be more appropriate to apply inductive approaches in order to study the theoretical theme that the data suggest (Saunders et al., 2009). This phenomenon is often seen in social studies and allows for a lot more variation and adjustments to theories as additional analysis of data can uncover more relationships or different causal influences than originally thought (Saunders et al., 2009). Inductive research is typically associated with qualitative data, allowing for many different views of the same phenomenon to be observed (Bryman & Bell, 2007).

Researchers can take full advantage of both approaches and apply both approaches together to complement each other (Jain & Sandhu, 2008). For example, induction can be used to generate and explain a theory where deduction can then be used to confirm the theory.

7.4 Data sources

Data are a fundamental aspect in all research studies, as every paper requires data to be analysed and interpreted in order to draw information and knowledge from them (Mingers, 2006). There are two types of data sources – primary and secondary – and they both have their advantages and disadvantages. Some researchers use both sources due to the availability of resources and to strengthen the reliability of data (Kuiper & Clippinger, 2012).

7.4.1 Secondary data

'Secondary data are data that have already been collected for purposes other than the problem at hand' (Malhotra, 2004, p.102), such as minutes of meetings, government surveys and daily newspapers. Secondary data can be quantitative or qualitative and may be raw data or compiled data. Raw data are data that do not undergo any processing or manipulation while compiled data are data that have been aggregated and summarised (Kervin, 1999). According to Saunders et al. (2007), there are three types of secondary data:

- Documentary data: include written materials, such as notices, books, journals and newspapers, and non-written materials, such as voice and video recordings, films, organisation databases. These data can be qualitative or quantitative and usually used along with primary data within a research study.
- Survey-based data: are usually collected through questionnaires using a survey strategy, such as censuses and ad hoc surveys. These collected data had an original purpose and often had been analysed.
- Multiple-source secondary data: a combination of data sets from different sources where such data can be purely documentary data or purely survey-based data, or a mixture of both types.

Secondary data often cannot provide all the information required in answering a research problem; however, secondary data could help to identify and define the research problem, develop a research approach and interpret primary data more comprehensively (Malhotra, 2004). There are many advantages to using secondary data in research studies and the major ones are as follows:

- Save resources, mostly time and money (Ghauri & Grønhaug, 2005), and therefore more economical.
- Much larger data sets can be obtained, especially if data are needed in a short period of time, secondary data is the only choice. This allows longitudinal studies to be carried out (Knight, 2008).
- Often higher quality than primary data and is an unobtrusive measure (Stewart & Kamins, 1993), since the data are already collected by organisations, such as governments or consultancy firms.

80 Research methodologies

Secondary data have been collected for a particular purpose by others, which leads to a few disadvantages:

- Data may have been collected for a different purpose to the research at hand (Denscombe 2007) and may have been presented subjectively to suit the original purpose.
- May not be appropriate for the research at hand due to the nature of the data and data collection methods (Saunders et al., 2007).
- Some may be difficult to assess due to confidential legal issues and some could be very costly, such as market research reports from Mintel (Saunders et al., 2007).
- No real control over the quality and accuracy of the data (Saunders et al., 2007).

7.4.2 Primary data

'Primary data are originated by a researcher for the specific purpose of addressing the research problem' (Malhotra, 2004, p.102). Malhotra (2004) and Kumar (2008) suggest that researchers should fully utilise and analyse secondary data before collecting primary data, as the amount of time and cost required can be large.

Observation

This method is fairly restricted and is often used to obtain information on people's behaviour as well as demographic and socioeconomic characteristics (Churchill & Lacobucci, 2005), therefore observation is usually used in descriptive research. Observations can be carried out by an individual or mechanical device, such as a video camera and people meters (Malhotra, 2004).

Communication

Interviews can be conducted in groups, one to one in person, or over the phone or via technological devices, depending on the standardisation and structure of the interviews (Malhotra, 2004). Non-standardised interviews, such as in-depth and semi-structured interviews are flexible and versatile allowing a detailed set of data to be collected (Saunders et al., 2007).

Advantages and disadvantages of observation compared to communication methods

The main advantage of observation is that there is no potential for reporting bias; the interviewee cannot be swayed or provide incorrect information (Saunders et al., 2007). Observation simply records actual events that cannot be disputed. On the other hand, observation is limited to recording events at face value; no inference or further information can be gathered from observation and no under-lying motives or preferences can be uncovered due to simply observing.

7.5 Data collection approach

The data collection approach can be classified in terms of quantitative collection or qualitative collection, by the characteristics of the data, data collection techniques and data analysis processes. Purely quantitative approaches, purely qualitative approaches or a combination of both approaches can be applied to a piece of research, depend-ing on the research objectives and resources available (Punch, 1998).

7.5.1 Quantitative data collection approach

Quantitative research 'is undertaken using a structured research approach with a sample of the population to produce quantifiable insights into behaviour, motiva-tions and attitudes' (Wilson, 2006, p.105). Quantitative research is often carried out by positivists who believe in scientific methods of gaining knowledge. Quantitative data are usually collected through questionnaire or observation where frequency of occurrences is recorded for quantitative purposes. The objectives of quantitative research are often to test hypotheses, determine relationships among variables, provide explanation and make predictions. This requires a large set of standardised data and statistical analysis (Johnson & Onwuegbuzie, 2004).

The advantages of quantitative research are:

- Data analysis is relatively easy and less time consuming with the use of statis-tical software.
- Statistically reliable.
- High precision gained from quantitative data.
- Research can be replicated.

The disadvantages of quantitative research are:

- Certain events or phenomena may be overlooked.
- Phenomena may not be understood if removed from their social environment (Bonoma, 1985).
- The structured nature of research and closed questions may lead to limited depth of results.

7.5.2 Qualitative data collection approach

Qualitative research is 'an unstructured research approach with a small number of carefully selected individuals to produce non-quantifiable insights into behaviour, motivations and attitudes' (Wilson, 2006, p.135). Qualitative research is often car-ried out by interpretivists who believe in the examination of experiences and

82 Research methodologies

feelings of social actors to gain knowledge. Qualitative data are often obtained through in-depth interview and focus groups, where emotions and experiences of interviewees freely expressed are captured (Jepson & Rodwell, 2008). The objective of qualitative research is to discover, explore and generate hypotheses or theories, from a small set of unstructured data and the interpretation of words (Johnson & Onwuegbuzie, 2004).

The advantages of qualitative research are (Babbie, 1986):

- Provides rich and detailed information in the research area.
- Allows flexibility in the data collection process, based on the issues that occur during the study.
- A small sample size is studied, which could mean less time and money is required.
- Useful in examining complex phenomena.

The disadvantages of qualitative research are (VanderStoep & Johnston, 2008):

- Validity and reliability are often criticised due to the subjectivity in data collection.
- Difficult to replicate and generalised.
- Lack of constituency due to its openness.
- Data analysis can be time consuming.

7.5.3 Mixed method approach

Both quantitative and qualitative research approaches have their own advantages and disadvantages leading to the development of the *fundamental principle of mixed research* by Turner (2003). This principle states the use of combinations or mixtures of qualitative and quantitative methods in such a way that the advantages of each method are maximised and complementary while the disadvantages of each method are counteracted by strength in the other (Turner, 2003; Brewer & Hunter, 1989).

Mixed methods research is 'the class of research where the researcher mixes or combines quantitative and qualitative research techniques, methods, approaches, concepts or language into a single study' (Johnson & Onwuegbuzie, 2004, p.17). There are two types of mixed methods research: mixed model and mixed method. Mixed model is the 'mixing of quantitative and qualitative approaches within or across the stages of the research process' (Johnson & Onwuegbuzie, 2004, p.20).

Data collected from one method can be analysed quantitatively and qualitatively. For example, data collection from questionnaires can provide both quantitative and qualitative data by including open-ended questions and ratings. In mixed model, researchers can take qualitative data and quantise it by converting it into a numerically significant format or taking quantitative data and discussing it qualitatively (Saunders et al., 2007). Mixed method refers to the application of both quantitative and qualitative approaches at the same time or sequentially in an overall research study (Johnson & Onwuegbuzie, 2004).

In mixed method, data are analysed separately according to the collection method, i.e. quantitative data are analysed quantitatively and qualitative data are analysed qualitatively, followed by the integration of findings at some stage (Johnson & Onwuegbuzie, 2004). In the process of mixed method research design, two major decisions must be made. Firstly, one must decide whether quantitative or qualitative procedures will predominate or if both will be used in equal measures. Then a decision of timing is made, whether to carry out quantitative and qualitative procedures simultaneously or sequentially.

According to the study of Greene et al. (1989), there are five main purposes in using mixed methods approaches:

- Triangulation: is the use of multiple research methods that take different perspectives, which can then be combined to create a single theory or interpretation of a phenomenon.
- Complementarity: uses results from one method to expand on and elaborate upon findings made by another, which is called complementarity.
- Development: uses a sequence of different methods in which results from the previous method are used to refine and focus the research.
- Initiation: analyses result from both quantitative and qualitative processes to find contradictions or paradoxes.
- Expansion: used for exploratory gain, expansion is the use of different methods to cover a wide scope of possible phenomena and uncover previously unrecognised events.

Mixed method research approaches raise philosophical issues associated with the research ontology and epistemology (Kuhn, 1963; Bryman, 1984; Howe, 1992), where qualitative purists hold the view of interpretivism and qualitative purists hold the view of positivism. Therefore, the 'accommodation between paradigms is impossible' (Guba, 1990, p.81), and qualitative and quantitative approaches cannot and should not be mixed. Most mixed method research holds the belief of pragmatism (Creswell, 2003), where approaches can be used in conjunction with the other effectively.

7.6 Data collection method

Firstly, the quantitative approach, the data mining technique, is used to generate association rules to capture the associations between items from a large set of transactional data. A qualitative approach using questionnaires is then followed to explore the results found previously, for example, the reasons behind association rules discovered. Therefore, the purpose of mixed method here is complementarity. The practice of mixed methods can be of great value in checking validity, accuracy and bias. It also allows for greater understanding of motives that bring about certain buying behaviour of consumers.

84 Research methodologies

Association rule mining is applied in this research where the main data required are 'items purchased in each transaction'. Large data sets allow interesting and unusual patterns to be discovered; therefore the ideal set of data to apply association rule mining to would be secondary data: a large database of customer transactions from the store being studied in this research. However, these transactional data are not accessible due to companies' confidentiality policies. The next most effective and accessible method is to carry out structured observation by the tills at the store, noting items purchased and the basket total of each single transaction to generate primary 'transactional data'.

A structured interview is considered a questionnaire, which is defined as 'all techniques of data collection in which each person is asked to respond to the same set of questions in a predetermined order' (Saunders et al., 2007, p.360). Due to the standardisation of questionnaires, this method is usually used in descriptive or explanatory research. Questionnaires can be self-administered, where the respondents complete questionnaires by themselves. Such questionnaires are often sent out through the internet, mail or in person (Malhotra, 2004). There are also interviewer-administered questionnaires where the interviewer records the set of answers from the respondent, and can be conducted as telephone questionnaires or as structured interviews in person (Malhotra, 2004).

Once the 'transactional data' have been analysed and association rules have been discovered, a self-administered questionnaire is then sent out via the internet to verify and explain the association rules found. The questionnaire consists of some opened and closed questions based on the findings from mining transactional data. The questionnaire is conducted over the internet, allowing a high diversity of questions and an ability to obtain sensitive information, such as monthly spending on fashion, with very low cost; however, response rates and levels of sample control are low (Malhotra, 2004).

7.7 Data analysis method

The data mining technique, association rule mining, is used to analyse the transactional data to discover the most frequent combination of items bought by customers and quantify the likelihood of such combinations (Giudici, 2003). The transactional data will be entered in a tabular data format in Microsoft Excel; each record represents a single transaction, with a '1' indicating items purchased and '0' indicating items not purchased. Data will then be analysed with the aid of statistical software, PASW Modeler 13, to generate the association rules and calculate the support, confidence and lift values. Association rule mining is used in this research to discover relationships between items because of its 'extreme simplicity and interpretational capacity' (Giudici, 2003, p.126).

There are no defined principles and rules for qualitative data analysis to generate meanings and draw conclusions (Miles & Huberman, 1994). The analysis procedure depends greatly on the level of creativity and how systematically one thinks (Patton, 1988). Denscombe (2007, p.288) summarised the qualitative process into five stages: *preparation of the data, familiarity with the data, interpreting the data, verifying the data* and *representing the data*. The manner in which these stages will be carried out in this research is described below:

- Preparation of the data: data will be grouped question by question, then typed and organised into tables with all the responses of one question grouped together.
- Familiarity with the data: data will be read thoroughly from different angles, bearing in mind any hidden meanings and preparing to identify appropriate codes.
- Interpreting the data: using template analysis, which involves developing codes, categorising information and coding the data. Then identification of any patterns, relationships and themes among the codes and categories and use of them to develop concepts and some generalised conclusions.
- Verifying the data: demonstrate the reliability and validity of the data.
- Representing the data: the major sections of data and data analysis procedure are presented with the answering of research objectives in mind.

7.7.1 Template analysis

Template analysis (King, 2004) is used in research to analyse qualitative data. During template analysis, 'researchers can develop codes only after some initial exploration of the data has taken place, using an immersion/ crystallisation or editing organising style. A common intermediate approach is when some initial codes are refined and modified during the analysis process' (Miller & Crabtree, 1999, p.167). Coding is the process of checking through all the data looking for themes, ideas and categories. Code labels are then used to mark sections of similar text for ease of reviewing when needed for comparison and analysis (Gibbs & Taylor, 2005).

Template analysis is highly flexible, since the template can be revised by adding new codes and reclassifying or deleting codes throughout the whole data collection and analysis process according to the needs of the research (King, 2004). This approach allows data to be managed in a structured manner, which helps to produce a clear and organised data representation. However, there is a lack of literature on template analysis compared to other approaches, such as grounded theory and discourse analysis, which can leave researchers with little guidance (Cassell & Symon, 2004). In addition, coding used in this approach may remove sections of text from their context. Template analysis will be used in the research to analyse the open-ended questions in the questionnaire.

7.8 Sampling and validation

Sampling techniques aim to increase efficiency of data collection by considering data from a sub-group rather than from all possible cases or elements. Sampling allows more practical data collection, where time and money usage can be

86 Research methodologies

minimised. There are two types of sampling techniques: probability sampling and non-probability sampling. Malhotra and Birks (2007, p.362) defined probability sampling as 'a sampling procedure in which each element of the population has a fixed probabilistic chance of being selected for the sample'. In this section of the study, a sample of the population is required to fill in an online questionnaire to verify and explain the association rules found from a set of transactional data. The ideal sampling method would be probability sampling with a sampling frame of the customer database of the store being studied; however, such a database is not accessible due to company confidentiality.

Validity is defined as 'the extent to which a measurement represents characteristics that exist in the phenomenon under investigation' (Malhotra & Birks, 2007, p.159), which refers to the accuracy, precision and appropriateness of the data. The transactional data are observed, recorded and entered into Excel with precision, so no errors arise. The association rule mining model developed in PASW Modeler 13 is also double checked to ensure the correct rules and values are generated. The validity of surveyed data is done by placing 'check questions' within the questionnaire deliberately to check for consistent responses to very similar questions (Denscombe, 2007). The validity of this piece of research is mostly achieved by the use of mixed method research approaches for triangulation, where findings can be corroborated and complemented. In addition, triangulation provides an opportunity to see phenomena from a different perspective, giving findings extra confidence as the same event is seen over a number of different data sets (Denscombe, 2007).

Reliability is 'the extent to which a scale produces consistent results if repeated measurements are made' (Malhotra, 2004, p.267). Repeatability of results provides safety in allowing researchers to rely on the results collected and be able to say results are free from random error. For results to be repeatable and reliable, the same results must be attainable from different, independent measurements (Churchill & Brown, 2007).

References

Arlbjørn, J.S. (1999). Logistik og supply chain management: Er der et teoretisk ståsted? (Logistics and Supply Chain Management: Is there a Theoretical Point of Departure?). *Ledelse & Erhvervsøkonomi*, 63(3), pp. 177–189.

Arlbjørn, J.S. & Halldórsson, A. (2002). Logistics knowledge creation: Reflections on content, context and processes. *International Journal of Physical Distribution & Logistics Management*, 32(1), pp. 22–40.

Babbie, E. (1986). *The practice of social research*, 4th ed. Belmont, CA: Wadsworth Publishing Co.

Bonoma, T.V. (1985). Case research in marketing: Opportunities, problems, and a process. *Journal of Marketing Research*, 22, May, pp. 199–208.

Brewer, J. & Hunter, A. (1989). *Multimethod research: A synthesis of styles*. Newbury Park, CA: Sage.

Bryan, D. & Gershman, A. (1999). Opportunistic Exploration of Large Consumer Product Spaces. *Proceedings of e-Commerce '99*, pp. 41–47.

Bryman, A. (1984). The Debate about Quantitative and Qualitative Research: A Question of Method or Epistemology. *The British Journal of Sociology*, 35(1), pp. 75–92.

Bryman, A. (2007). *Social Research Methods*. New York, NY: Oxford University Press.

Bryman, A. & Bell, E. (2007). *Business Research Methods*. New York, NY: Oxford University Press.

Cassell, C.M. & Symon, G. (2004). *Essential Guide to Qualitative Methods in Organizational Research*. London: Sage Publications.

Chia, R. (2002). 'The Production of Management Knowledge: Philosophical Underpinnings of Research Design', in D. Partington (ed.), *Essential Skills for Management Research*, 1st edn. London: SAGE Publications Ltd, pp. 1–19.

Churchill, G.A. & Brown, T.J. (2007). *Basic Marketing Research*. Mason, OH: Thomson South-Western.

Churchill, G.A. Jr & Lacobucci, D. (2005). *Marketing Research: Methodological Foundations*, 9th edn. Mason, OH: Thomson Learning.

Crabtree, B.F. & Miller, W.L. (1999). *Doing Qualitative Research*. Sage.

Creswell, J.W. (2003). *Research Design: Quantitative, Qualitative, and Mixed Methods Approaches*. Thousand Oaks, USA: Sage.

Crotty, M. (1998). *The Foundations of Social Research: Meaning and Perspective in the Research Process*. London: Sage.

Daymon, C. & Holloway, I. (2011). *Qualitative Research Methods in Public Relations and Marketing Communications*. London: Routledge.

Denscombe, M. (2007). *The Good Research Guide: For Small-scale Social Research Projects*. Maidenhead, England; New York: Open University Press.

Dietz, J.L.G. (2006). *Enterprise Ontology: Theory and Methodology*. Springer.

Easterby-Smith, M., Thorpe, R. & Lowe, A. (1997). *Management Research: An Introduction*. London: Sage.

Easterby-Smith, M., Thorpe, R. & Jackson, P. (2008). *Management Research*. London: SAGE.

Ellram, L.M. (1996). The Use of the Case Study Method in Logistics Research. *Journal of Business Logistics*, 17(2), pp. 93–138.

Gammelgaard, B. (1997). 'A Joint-Nordic Ph.D. Program in Logistics', in J. Masters (ed.), *Proceedings of The Twenty-Sixth Annual Transportation and Logistics Educators Conference*. Chicago: Council of Logistics Management.

Garver, M.S. & Mentzer, J.T. (1999). Logistics Research Methods Employing Structural Equation Modeling to Test for Construct Validity. *Journal of Business Logistics*, 20(1), pp. 33–57.

Ghauri, P.N. & Grønhaug, K. (2005). *Research Methods in Business Studies: A Practical Guide*, 3rd edn. London: Prentice-Hall.

Gibbs, G.R. & Taylor, C. (2005). *How and What to Code* [online]. Available at: http://onlineqda.hud.ac.uk/Intro_QDA/how_what_to_code.php [accessed 6 March 2017].

Giudici, P. (2003). *Applied Data Mining: Statistical Methods for Business and Industry*. Chichester: Wiley.

Greene, J.C., Caracelli, V.J. & Graham, W.F. (1989). Toward a conceptual framework for mixed-method evaluation designs. *Educational Evaluation and Policy Analysis*, 11(3), pp. 255–274.

Guba, E.G. (1990). *The Paradigm Dialog*. Newbury Park, CA: Sage Publications.

Guba, E.G. & Lincoln, Y.S. (1994). 'Competing paradigms in qualitative research', in N.K. Denzin & Y.S. Lincoln (eds), *Handbook of Qualitative Research*. London: Sage, pp. 105–117.

Howe, K. (1992). Getting Over the Quantitative-Qualitative Debate. *American Journal of Education*, 100(2), pp. 236–256.

Jepsen, D.M. & Rodwell, J.J. (2008). Convergent interviewing: A qualitative diagnostic technique for researchers. *Management Research News*, 31(9), pp. 650–658.

88 Research methodologies

Jones, M.A., Reynolds, K.E. & Arnold, M.J. (2006). Hedonic and utilitarian shopping value: Investigating differential effects on retail outcomes. *Journal of Business Research*, 59(9), pp. 974–981.

Kervin, J.B. (1999). *Methods for Business Research*, 2nd edn. MB: Manitoba Teachers' Society.

King, N. (2004). 'Template analysis', in C.M. Cassell & G. Symon (eds), *Essential Guide to Qualitative Methods in Organizational Research*. London: Sage Publications.

Knight, S.A. (2008). *User perceptions of information quality in World Wide Web information retrieval behaviours*. PhD Dissertation, School of Management Information Systems, Edith Cowan University, Perth Western, Australia.

Kuhn, T.S. (1963). 'The essential tension: Tradition and innovation in scientific research', in C.W. Taylor & F. Barron (eds), *Scientific Creativity: Its Recognition and Development*. NY: Wiley, pp. 341–354.

Kuiper, S. & Clippinger, D. (2012). *Contemporary Business Reports*. USA: South-Western College Pub.

Kumar, C.R. (2008). *Research Methodology*. India: APH Publishing Corporation.

Jain, T.R. & Sandhu, A.S. (2008). *Macroeconomics*. India: V K Publications.

Johnson, R.B. & Onwuegbuzie, A.J. (2004). Mixed methods research: A research paradigm whose time has come. *Educational Researcher*, 33(7), pp. 14–26.

Jones, M.A., Reynolds, K.E., Weun, S. & Beatty, S.E. (2003). The product-specific nature of impulse buying tendency. *Journal of Business Research*, 56(7), pp. 505–511.

Malhotra, N.K. (2004). *Marketing Research: An applied orientation*, 4th edn. Upper Saddle River, NJ: Prentice Hall.

Malhotra, N. & Birks, D. (2007). *Marketing Research: An applied approach*, 3rd European edn. Harlow, UK: Pearson Education.

Marsh, D. & Furlong, P. (2002). 'A Skin not a Sweater: Ontology and Epistemology in Political Science', in David Marsh & Gerry Stoker (eds), *Theories and Methods of Political Science*, 2nd edn. Basingstoke: Palgrave, pp. 17–41.

Mentzer, J.T. & Flint, D.J. (1997). Validity in Logistics Research. *Journal of Business Logistics*, 18(2), pp. 199–216.

Mentzer, J.T. & Kahn, K. (1995). A Framework for Logistics Research. *Journal of Business Logistics*, 16(1), pp. 231–250.

Miles, M.B. & Huberman, A.M. (1994). *Qualitative Data Analysis*. Thousand Oaks, CA: Sage Publications.

Miller, W.L. & Crabtree, B.F. (1999). 'Clinical research: A multi-methods and qualitative road map', in B.F. Crabtree & W.L. Miller (eds), *Doing Qualitative Research*, 2nd edn. Thousand Oaks, CA: Sage.

Mingers, J. (2006). Intelligent thinking instead of critical realism? Response from the author: Intelligence and realism in OR. *Journal of the Operational Research Society*, 57, pp. 1375–1379.

Näslund, D. (2002). Logistics Needs Qualitative Research – Especially Action Research. *International Journal of Physical Distribution & Logistics Management*, 32(5), pp. 321–338.

Patton, M. (1988). 'Paradigms and pragmatism', in D. Fetterman (ed.), *Qualitative Approaches to Evaluation in Educational Research*. Thousand Oaks, CA: Sage, pp. 116–137.

Punch, K. (1998). *Introduction to Social Research: Quantitative and Qualitative Approaches*. London: Sage.

Saunders, M., Lewis, P. & Thornhill, A. (2007). *Research Methods for Business Students*, 4th edn. London: Prentice Hall.

Saunders, M., Lewis, P. & Thornhill, A. (2009). *Research Methods for Business Students*, 5th edn. Harlow: Financial Times Prentice Hall.

Seaker, R.F., Waller, M.A. & Dunn, S.C. (1993). A Note on Research Methodology in Business Logistics. *Logistics and Transportation Review*, 29(4), pp. 383–387.

Stewart, D.W. & Kamins, M.A. (1993). *Secondary research: Information sources and methods.* Sage.

Tashakkori, A. & Teddlie, C. (1998). *Mixed methodology: Combining qualitative and quantitative approaches.* Applied Social Research Methods, No. 46. Thousand Oaks, CA: Sage.

Trochim, W.M. (2006). *Web Centre of Social Research Method* [online]. Available at: www. socialresearchmethods.net/kb/philosophy.php [accessed 6 March 2017].

Turner, D.S. (2003). Horizons revealed: From methodology to method. *International Journal of Qualitative Methods.*

VanderStoep, S.C. & Johnston, D.D. (2008). *Research Methods for Everyday Life: Blending Qualitative and Quantitative Approaches.* Jossey-Bass Wiley US.

Voss, C., Tsikriktsis, N. & Frolich, M. (2002). Case Research in Operations Management. *International Journal of Operations & Production Management*, 22(2), pp. 195–218.

Wilson, A. (2006). *Marketing research: An integrated approach*, 2nd edn. Gosport: Prentice Hall; York: Springer.

8

SOCIAL MEDIA AND THE FASHION SUPPLY CHAIN

Collaboration using social communication technologies enables members of the supply chain to work better together, coordinating their operational activities and making improvements (Taylor, 2015). This collaboration can involve all levels of an organisation to better coordinate their efforts to achieve supply chain performance goals (Montpetit, 2015; Lau, 2016). Social media can be a tool to enable such coordination. Social media have been used mostly by business-to-consumer to enable enterprises to promote their brands and market their products to consumers (Howells, 2011). In this chapter, theories and literature about social media, fashion blogs, fast fashion and the luxury market, and brand image will be discussed.

8.1 Social media

Kaplan and Haenlein (2010, p.61) defined social media as 'internet-based applications that build on the ideological and technical foundations of Web 2.0, and that allow the creation and exchange of user generated content'. All the information concerning products, services and brands provided and spread through social media are created, circulated and used by consumers to influence other consumers (Murugesan, 2007). It is a communication mechanism through which users could communicate with people from any place at any time (Williams et al., 2012). Social media platforms are usually inexpensive or free to use, such as blogs, Facebook, YouTube, LinkedIn, Twitter and others. Social media are a critical area of interest for marketing scholars and practitioners. According to recent research, over 80% of marketers have taken social media as a practical tool and every year over US$60 billion are invested in social media for advertising activities (Gil-Or, 2010; Smith, 2011). It is reasonable to claim that social media signal a revolutionary trend, and generate interest for companies operating in digital space (Sedeke, 2012).

Contact is a great convenience and benefit that social media bring to both consumers and fashion brands, and it will show its advantage in the long run (Okazaki et al., 2007). The rules and patterns of business have been altered because of the emergence of social media, and communication and dissemination of information have also been changed. Because of internet-based media, people are able to communicate with thousands of other people online. Kaplan and Haenlein (2010) think that social media can be beneficial in business because of their direct and in-time communication characteristics. Compared to traditional communication tools, social media have a relatively low cost and a higher level of efficiency. It is predicted that social media will be a critical part of the future of virtual communication.

8.2 Fashion industry and social media

Fashion usually reflects actual lifestyle, trends and developments of society. Because of the development of the internet and digital technologies, the fashion industry has been influenced and changed to a great extent. It has transformed the industry operation environment, and has made it more global, direct and interactive (Sedeke, 2012). Under this global and digital background, current fashion marketers need to incorporate social media as a tool of publicity and communication. Guzelis (2010) said it is quite important for brands to learn and to develop the ability of influencing what and how people think, which means people's attitude towards a product or brand. Then the company could find out how these consumers' buying decisions will be affected and they can take advantage of it.

Social media encourage customers to have an active interaction with brands, which could help build the brand and promote it by increasing brand awareness, involvement and engagement, to stimulate a desire to purchase. Though at first many fashion brands claimed that social networking is not helpful for the relationship development between brands and consumers, it is becoming a very important channel for customer relationship improvement. And it could help to expand audience base (Mohr, 2013).

Word of mouth and viral marketing are the two main ways for social media to boost interest in the fast fashion market and luxury market. Word of mouth could spread information about products and services among consumers, which has already become a very influential source for consumers (Arndt, 1967; Alreck & Settle, 1995).

The narrative power and the ability to generate stories are two typical characteristics of blogging (Woodside et al., 2008). Bloggers normally relate their consumption experiences by carefully organising the story in ways that the blog readers may find appealing and interesting in order to attract more visitors and increase traffic (Arsel & Zhao, 2010). Blog posts consist of pictures, videos and other multimedia content. Generally, most blogs contain hypertext links leading to other websites. Personal blogs, as the most popular blogs, share bloggers' experiences, opinions and feelings (Knoll & Bronstein, 2014). Therefore, blog

92 Social media and the fashion supply chain

visitors are an important factor on deciding how and what consumers write in some ways.

Nardi et al. (2004) explore the reasons why people blog and come up with five general motives: to document life, express inside emotions, form community, provide opinions and articulate ideas through writing. Meanwhile Boram (2010) thought that self-reflection is the first motivation for bloggers to blog. People tend to reflect their identities through possessions, social and symbolic affiliations (Belk, 1998). Within the community of blogging, individuals are able to build associations with products, brands, and don't have to actually possess them, and it is a new means of self-extension by creating an ideal self (Schau & Gilly, 2003). And they further claim that the increased blogging experience is helpful for expanding audience numbers. In addition, the motivations for blogging are getting more complicated at the same time and can be divided into two categories: digital engagement and e-shopping blogging behaviour. Digital engagement refers to the action to produce information that could further lead to positive feedback and then to active social interactions.

Shao (2008) claims engagement and time efficiency are important characteristics of blogging. A blog is a platform that is time efficient and easy to use, and it is multidirectional communication, which is appreciated by most users since people get less free time now. Additionally, it brings high interactivity by offering a platform to encourage discussion and sharing (Kuhn, 2007).

Brand use practice is a type of generic value-creation practice. According to several pieces of research, brand use practices refer to customising and so on for the purpose of improving the use of a brand. However, there is the opposite point that focusing on brands will limit the study of community. Community relies on external resources as well and various consumption objects should be used to create an 'in the know' ambience (Ostberg, 2007).

8.3 Fashion blogging

This research aims to study brand community based on personal style. According to Muniz and O'Guinn (2001), there are three attributes of social community – a shared consciousness, rituals and traditions, and a sense of moral responsibility. This chapter will show the formalisation of a virtual community based on a shared interest in style, and learn about how different style sets are adopted by using different fashion brands within the communities. In the following section, the research will focus on the function of brand community, personal style and the relation between them, and look at how these blogs drive consumers' buying behaviour and preference, and the way blogs build and promote brand image.

Because of the development of the internet, fashion is everywhere now. Most people have access to learning information about fashion. Fashion blogs provide consumers with a free and almost unlimited space to express themselves on the internet, which is called self-expression (Kozinets, 2006). Fashion blogs always ensure new fashion trends and information are updated regularly by the bloggers to provide information access to consumers. Blog readers can learn the latest looks from fashion bloggers as well as share their favourites. This unique engaging experience gives consumers a chance to express their opinions (Mohr, 2013).

Fashion is an ongoing changing process and a product of the time (Easey, 2009). Currently, more people tend to live in a fashionable way. Being 'fashionable' requires keeping up to date with the latest fashion information; the places a person goes and the people they communicate with also determine the fashionable level. Fashion used to be greatly privileged and highly costly to access. However, now it is more accessible and democratised because of the emergence of digital technology, and people are able to participate in this specific area without any material limitations.

In fashion business, it is more common for a blogger to mention a certain brand in a positive way, the brand will send the blogger their product for free to show appreciation and to encourage the blogger to continue. This is a demonstration of good and efficient marketing strategy (Sedeke, 2012). Guzelis (2010) pointed out that people would discuss with each other about what they are interested in and actively interact through this platform, which suggests the power of blogging is information sharing. And it also stresses some important factors of this medium – awareness, participation and engagement. Fashion bloggers are extremely influential in the current environment. Brands have learned that fashion bloggers have a great influence to turn readers into consumers. Taking Coach as an example, it worked with four bloggers in 2010 on limited-edition Coach bags. These bloggers participate in the design process and it represents their idea and hard work, so they promote these bags through blogging (Griffith, 2011).

Besides expressing actual and ideal self through self-narrative, taste display, and brand and style reveal, blogging could serve as a communication platform to help form a community by connecting bloggers together with blog readers online and produce an impact on others' views. According to Grunig and Grunig (1995), a fashion blog is a 'two-way communication', by which it means blog readers and blogger could communicate and express their opinion at any time and any place. Fashion blogging provides a voice for the public. On one hand, fashion bloggers could share their insights and thoughts on this platform. The designers and press get information and inspiration from these voices and create products based on these (Durmaz, 2014). Even between bloggers and their readers there is two-way communication. Nichols pointed out that bloggers are becoming more important as they provide consumers with an inside look into the latest trends and styles; they are resources for blog readers (Nichols, 2010). At the same time, a blogger receives feedback and gets inspiration from blog readers through media and comments. A fashion blogger could create a connection and receive feedback from their audience. This connection could help the blogger create credibility and grow their reader base. If a blogger wants to become more influential within the online community, it is necessary to build strong relationships with blog followers and other trusted bloggers as well (Redsicker, 2013). Besides, bloggers need to evaluate the status of their readership, and also gain readership by spreading their content by utilising all kinds of social media sites, both traditional and upcoming, to create more traffic to their blogs and expand the consumer base. Use of social media like

Facebook, Twitter, Instagram and so on to lead readers back to their blogs is one common method for bloggers to increase readership.

Consumer engagement and fashion involvement are two important elements for online fashion business. Normally, compared with other regular consumers, engaged consumers are more loyal and connected to a brand or a community (Brodie et al., 2011). Therefore, fashion brands need to get brand consumers engaged to try to keep consumers' loyalty. And active consumer engagement is becoming essential to develop a unique competitive advantage for the company under this digital background (Raeis & Lingjie, 2017). Fashion blogging encourages consumer engagement by active interaction with brand consumers through this platform, which could help promote this fashion blog and fashion brands in this blog. Apparel is a product with a high level of involvement, it needs to be seen, tried on and touched, given its special characteristics (Workman, 2010). The in-store experience has transferred to online experience because of technology advancement. High involvement characteristics are shown through virtual try-on, object interactivity, mix and match and so on. Obviously the interactivity of products will contribute to consumer engagement level, and the expansion of fashion blogging and improvement of the online shopping experience (Perry et al., 2013). Fashion blogging secures that consumers enjoy a high level of engagement. Accordingly, highly engaged consumers will show higher loyalty, connection, trust and commitment to a brand (Brodie et al., 2011). The study of fashion communities not only can provide some implications for marketers in the fashion industry, but more importantly, it explains how communities form based on sets of brands.

Blogging in some way also causes ineffective communication. Despite blogging encouraging a two-way communication, overloaded information costs people too much time spent on selecting information. And it causes bad quality and less value of information (Wang, 2011). David (2008, p.87) identified the concept of fragmentation: 'the shift during the life span of knowledge management from the "chunked" material of case studies and best-practice documents to the unstructured, fragmented and finely granular material that pervades the blogosphere'.

Mangold and Faulds (2009) argued that social media are part of the promotion mix based on current developments: companies need to talk and communicate with their customers, while customers can talk directly to others and interact with fashion brands. 'Even though the content, timing, and frequency of social media conversations are outside of the managers' control, they must learn how to shape consumers' discussions in a manner that is consistent with the organization's mission and performance goals' (Mangold & Faulds, 2009, p.358). According to Mangold and Faulds, blogs should be seen as an opportunity as well, a challenge instead of a threat.

Identity refers to the way of presenting or expressing ourselves to other people, guidance for people's interaction and behaviour towards other people. There is a visual communication way to express our identities through fashion, which shows who we are by what we wear and how we wear it. What we wear and how we choose to dress have psychological, political, economic, and social meanings and consequences (Sika, 2014). Identity is a complex concept that can be interpreted as a different set of meanings that define a person in society (Burke, 1980). Many scholars claim that people possess multiple identities. Social, role and personal identity are three widely accepted basic identities. The overall identities of people normally are a blend of these three. The roles of people in society dictate their identities, and identities in turn prescribe people's feelings, thoughts and general behaviours. Identities are linked to society, and one can hardly be understood when outside society. As for personal identities, these are more closely tied to individuals compared with social and role identities (Burke & Stets, 2000). To discuss how fashion shapes people's identity, it is necessary to study in which ways that fashion has shaped people's social, role and personal identities. The way people choose to present themselves proclaims the identity they enact or embody (Sika, 2014).

Mixing and matching different brands helps consumers to aestheticise self-creation and to display multiple identities, and consumers' attention is drawn to what product conveys through image and identity, not only focus on brands (Wattanasuwan, 2005). Since blogging has become a huge phenomenon, it even changes fashion consumption in some way. Managing a successful blog is not easy; it requires putting a lot of time and effort into providing unique and valuable content to satisfy the audience (Sedeke, 2012). As mentioned earlier, fashion bloggers have changed people's daily life and expanded the possibilities for self-presentation greatly (Llamas & Belk, 2013). And fashion bloggers will create ideal imagined characters; these bloggers project identities that fit the surrounding environment, consumer values and current fashion trend (Zhao & Belk, 2007). In addition, fashion bloggers will tell a story that includes content that could feature brands and products (Kretz, 2010), and exaggerate or try to nurture the character they have in mind to meet the audience's need (Schau & Gilly, 2003). Moreover, the narrative of consumption is helpful to construct the blogger's identity and to generate empathy, which would lead to an increase in the influence of the fashion blogger among their audience. Therefore, fashion bloggers prefer to display the brands and products that their readers like (Llamas & Belk, 2013).

At the beginning, the blog is usually anonymous. However, the anonymity phenomenon has declined and as more bloggers try to disclose identity, they start paying more attention to personal branding in their blogs. Currently, bloggers make an effort to manage their blogs as a personal brand, which means the blog's name could even equal a brand's name; by reading the content people could learn of a certain personality a blog represents and expresses, and the virtual extended self a brand constructs (Kretz, 2010). Put another way, right now fashion blogs are entitled with strong personalities compared with before. Brand personality is a primary component when it comes to building brand image along with other elements (Maehle & Shneor, 2010). As personal brands, fashion blogs have extended their reach to a much wider range of readers. And by linking their blogs to social networking media like Facebook, Instagram, Lookbook, Pinterest, YouTube and so on, fashion bloggers could maintain their visibility by publishing content at a regular and fast pace (Llamas & Belk, 2013). There are more and more people who will follow the trend and purchase products shown in blogs. Llamas and Belk (2013) said that not only do we consume blogs, but we also consume through blogs. The power in the fashion market has been shifting gradually from marketer to consumer because of the increased influence of fashion blogging (Llamas & Belk, 2013). One problem caused by fashion blogging is that as readers tend to follow the bloggers, fashion is getting more boring because more people tend to follow a similar trend and they are losing their own personalities and ability to create their own fashion style (Wei, 2009).

8.4 Social media and fashion markets

8.4.1 Social media and the fast fashion market

Fast fashion and luxury brands are two different markets. In this section, the concepts and characteristics of the fast fashion market and luxury market will be studied, and further analysis of the influence of fashion blogs on their brand image building will be done as well.

Fast fashion refers to clothing collections based on the latest fashion trends. Fast fashion is a product of an ongoing changing fashion market; it is a new phenomenon and new trend in a competitive market. As the fashion cycle is moving faster than before, and with the advantage of the internet and technology, fashion information updates more rapidly and forms a new market, which is different from the traditional fashion market. Unlike the haute couture or luxury fashion retailers, fast fashion retailers do not invest too much in design. They are more likely to be inspired by the latest and attractive trends they observed in fashion shows (Agins, 1999; Reinach, 2005). Fast fashion retailers turn these new trends into products, which they can sell on the market as soon as possible (Reinach, 2005). Currently, fast fashion retailers are required to improve their store numbers and maximise the speed (Tokatli, 2007). Fast fashion brands like Zara and H&M had around 1,444 and 2,000 stores, respectively, by 2010. Furthermore, most fast fashion retailers put an emphasis on selecting new designs, transforming these designs into profitable products immediately (Chen et al., 2005).

Fast fashion has a shorter cycle. Short production times and lead times, highly efficient supply chain systems and product design that follows the latest fashion are the special characteristics of fast fashion (Cachon & Swinney, 2009). There is a shared feature between fast fashion and fashion blogging in that they are both new products of the changing fashion market. In the fashion industry, the whole process from production to distribution can be de-localised, which makes products cheaper than in other industries (Bosshart, 2006). Making fashion democratised with lower prices is the key feature of fast fashion – that is to say cheap is an important advantage for fast fashion brands. Fast fashion is unable to compete with luxury fashion in quality or design.

Quick response capabilities with excellent product design capabilities are the guarantee of a successful fast fashion system, so that trendy products could be designed and minimal production lead time can be guaranteed to match supply (Cachon & Swinney, 2009).

Generally, fast fashion is proven to be low level of involvement products, which means fast fashion consumers have a weak motivation to process information. Low involvement usually is a disadvantage for marketers, because a lower involvement level means more effort is needed to be put into the product information process (Arndt, 1967). Thus, a fashion company needs to make an effort to get higher-level involvement, which is necessary for its success. For example, preparing free fashion magazines in stores to attract potential consumers or fans. Social media help boost interest through word of mouth both in the fast fashion market and luxury market. Word of mouth could spread information about products and services among consumers, which makes a great influence on consumers (Arndt, 1967; Alreck & Settle, 1995).

Brand is a valuable asset for most fashion companies (THREAD, 2009). Brand value is one critical part of advertising. Companies that understand the significance of brand value and as well are capable of taking advantage of brand value could distinguish themselves from other fashion brands in the market. Furthermore, realising the reaction of customers to brands is important for companies to make a strategic plan. Brands carry different roles. A highly recognised brand helps boost sales. A number of consumers would like to pay more money for the brand name, as it is a symbol of social status and identity. Also many consumers care more about brands so that those people would choose a product based on the brand instead of style. It conveys a kind of personality (Kapferer, 1997). Personal style is a way to show who you are. The dressing style could convey an individual's preference and personality in some way (Malik, 2015).

Despite the current situation, the higher level of fashion a city enjoys, the weaker people's attention and dependence on the brand logo as there is no need to prove anything with brand in these cities that have a high level of fashion. But this is not common to all cities (O'Reilly, 2015).

8.4.2 Social media and the luxury fashion market

The concept of luxury has a long history. Luxury goods have always been associated with power, wealth, exclusivity and satisfaction as well. According to most experts, luxury refers to a conceptual and symbolic dimension instead of specific products, which are strongly characterised with the cultural values of the society within a particular historical period. Therefore, they define that luxury is what could create a more comfortable, enjoyable and fulfilling life (Danziger, 2005).

Luxury goods are made with the purpose of impressing others by signalling wealth and conspicuous consumption instead of being consumed because of their intrinsic value (Dubois & Paternault, 1995; Piccione & Rubinstein, 2008). Prendergast et al. (2000) identified that luxury cannot be defined based on price. Other scholars like Dubois and Czellar (2002) also disagree with taking price as the most important factor when buying luxuries. Perceived high cost is a necessary for luxury goods but not a sufficient condition. Besides high price, excellent quality and specialised distribution channels are also important elements to define luxury brands (Kapferer, 2001).

At present, luxury is everywhere and everyone wants to consume luxury products, which attracts consumption and leads to profits. Luxury retailing has different characteristics from other retail sectors in three important ways. First of all, most luxury retailers themselves manufacture goods instead of a third party. This means that what and how they sell their products are linked (Mores, 2007). The second characteristic of luxury retailers is as the most prolific: many luxury retailers operate retail stores worldwide. Third, when it comes to foreign market entry, more luxury retailers use direct investment as a method (Mores, 2007). A flagship store is crucial to these characteristics of luxury retailing. In international markets, a flagship is the primary form of direct investment when entering into a foreign market and it promotes brand growth in both domestic and foreign markets (Moore & Docherty, 2007). Flagship stores encourage representation and distribution by third parties, which secures interest and engagement among consumers.

Fashion blogging could provide what consumers are looking for (Corda, 2012). Another reason that the luxury market should take advantage of social media is that a luxury brand is always seen as the leader in the fashion industry in all aspects: the product itself, and management and novel value as well, which is the key point to secure profit. To survive the fierce competition and changing environment, luxury brands need to turn to marketing communication by using social media. These two-way communication platforms allow users to interact with others online. The use of these platforms has expanded to the majority of luxury fashion brands so far and is quite helpful for business development. According to research, the use of social media like fashion blogging could help create closer, satisfactory and interactive relationships with users, provide customised service and entertainment content.

8.5 Brand image building

Brand management scholars claim that brand image is essential for building powerful brands, which helps brands differentiate their products from other competitors (e.g. Aaker, 1996; Kapferer, 1997). Brand image refers to brand association (Koubaa, 2008). It is the perceptions consumers hold about a brand reflected by brand associations (Herzog, 1963). Dobni and Zinkhan (1990) argued that brand image is the result of interaction between the receiver and the product stimuli. There are several factors contributing to brand image building, which are product attributes, the marketing mix, the firm, individual perceptions, personal values, brand user type, and context variables. Brand image is of great importance in the realm of marketing, but a lack of theory development results in much ambiguity about brand image and brand personality (Patterson, 1999).

Creative design skills and identification with customer preferences are two essential criteria for fashion as continual change process. Design skills are about talent. Identification with customers refers to marketing that ensures the creative component could be used to the best advantage, and increase the possibility for business to succeed and grow. Easey (2009) claims that because the fashion industry is a changing process, fashion marketing practices are slightly different compared with other marketing areas. Beside the above two factors, a strong brand image is another essential component concerning fashion marketing. The success of a fashion brand is greatly dependent on how much it understands its target consumer needs and creates new wants. The symbols carried by a fashion product are called 'silent language'. It is important for fashion marketers to figure out why consumers chose one brand over another and the reasons behind that. As Lee et al. (2009) point out, the reason why people talk about different brands in different ways, and why or why not they buy its products, are all because of brand image to some extent. Image is more than a name, logo, slogan and design. It is more like a whole concept that contains symbolic meaning, ideas, attitudes and more about this brand. For example, the brand Levi's has developed urban-hip user imagery more than just a label in youngsters' minds (Lee et al., 2009). The fashion market has a strong dependence on creating and maintaining a desirable and distinctive image, which brings additional value and brand differentiation. According to Hitt et al. (2009), to achieve competitive advantage by differentiating a brand from its competitors is the main goal for fashion marketing. Differentiation usually can be based on products, or services or other aspects but in the fashion industry, differentiation is more about overall brand image.

The lack of copyright protection is another reason why brands should build a strong image. In the fashion industry, there is no intellectual property protection. Basically anybody could copy any design from others, make a little change and then present it as their own (Blakley, 2010). This situation is especially obvious in the fast fashion industry. The lack of legislative coverage as well as the ongoing pressure is the character of the fashion industry. Designers of haute couture usually gain inspiration from other culture fields, like music and the film industry; sometimes from street fashion or even vintage collections. This mechanism leads to the democratisation of the fashion industry (Blakley, 2010). Given the key characteristics of contemporary fashion, fashion marketing is a management process involved in anticipating, identifying and satisfying customer demands to meet the organisation's long-term goals, and continuously build or maintain a strong brand image. To achieve those goals, common techniques such as branding, pricing and so on are needed (Easey, 2009). What is more, as a new set of platforms, social media like blogging are also necessary. It can build an authentic relationship with consumers and help fashion brands to create a favourable brand image.

References

Aaker, D.A. (1996). *Building Strong Brands*. New York, NY: The Free Press.
Agins, T. (1999). *The End of Fashion: How Marketing Changed the Clothing Industry Forever*. New York: Quill.
Alreck, P.L. & Settle, R.B. (1995). The importance of word-of-mouth communications to service buyers. *Proceedings of American Marketing Association* (Winter), pp. 188–193.

100 Social media and the fashion supply chain

Arndt, J. (1967). Role of product-related conversations in the diffusion of a new product. *Journal of Marketing Research*, 4(3), pp. 291–295.

Arsel, Z. & Zhao, X. (2010). 'Personal Blogging, Performance and the Quest for Fame', in D.W. Dahl, G.V. Johar & S.M.J. van Osselaer (eds), *Advances in Consumer Research*, vol. 38. Duluth, MN: Association for Consumer Research.

Belk, R.W. (1998). Professions and the Extended Self. *Journal of Consumer Research* [online]. Available at: www.aber.ac.uk/en/media/training/beforesept14/samwindows/pdf/belk-et-al-%281988%29-%27extended-self%27%281%29.pdf [accessed 18 February 2017].

Blakley, J. (2010). *Johanna Blakley: Lessons from fashion's free culture*. Video. Available at: http://tinyurl.com/nl5m693 [accessed 2 November 2017].

Boram, J. (2010). Makers of Dy'd, Fancy and Japan'd Chairs. *Regional Furniture*, xxiv, pp. 70–75.

Bosshart, D. (2006). *Cheap: The Real Cost of the Global Trend for Bargains, Discounts & Consumer Choice*. London: Kogan Page Ltd.

Brodie, R.J., Ilic, A., Juric, B. & Hollebeek, L. (2011). Consumer engagement in a virtual brand community: An exploratory analysis. *Journal of Business Research* [online]. Available at: www.sciencedirect.com/science/article/pii/S0148296311002657 [accessed 18 April 2016].

Burke, P.J. (1980). The self: Measurement implications from a symbolic interactionist perspective. *Social Psychology Quarterly*, 43, pp. 18–29.

Burke, P.J. & Stets, J.E. (2000). Identity theory and social identity theory. *Social Psychology Quarterly*, 63(3), pp. 224–237.

Cachon, P.G. & Swinney, R. (2009). *The Value of Fast Fashion: Rapid Production, Enhanced Design, and Strategic Consumer Behavior* [online]. Available at: http://opim.wharton.upenn.edu/~cachon/pdf/FastFashion_Final.pdf [accessed 18 April 2015].

Chen, Y., Das, S., Dellarocas, C., Pfeiffer, B. et al. (2005). The Firm's Management of Social Interactions. *Marketing Letters*, 16(3/4), pp. 415–428 [online]. Available at: http://link.springer.com/article/10.1007/s11002-005-5902-4 [accessed 10 August 2015].

Corda (2012). 'Greening Your Business', Colchester Regional Development Authority. Available at: www.corda.ca/greenbusiness/ [accessed January 2018].

Danziger, P. (2005). *Let Them Eat Cake: Marketing Luxury to the Masses – As Well as the Classes*. Chicago: Dearborn Trade Publishing, pp. 50–56.

David, K. & Yang, S. (2008). *Social network analysis*. CA: SAGE Publications.

Dobni, D. & Zinkhan, G.M. (1990). 'In search of brand image: A foundation analysis', in M. E. Goldberg, G. Gorn & R.W. Pollay (eds), *Advances in Consumer Research*, Vol. 17. New Orleans, LA: Association of Consumer Research.

Dubois, B. & Czellar, S. (2002). Prestige brands or luxury brands? An exploratory inquiry on consumer perceptions. *Marketing in a Changing World: Scope, Opportunities and Challenges: Proceedings of the 31st EMAC Conference*, University of Minho, Portugal, 28–31 May.

Dubois, B. & Paternault, C. (1995). Observations: Understanding the world of international luxury brands: the 'dream formula'. *Journal of Advertising Research*, 35(4), pp. 69–76.

Durmaz, L. (2014). *The Role of Social Media in the Fashion Industry: How Fashion Blogging Encourages Two-way Symmetrical Communication* [online]. Available at: http://digitalcommons.calpoly.edu/cgi/viewcontent.cgi?article=1081&context=joursp [accessed 18 April 2015].

Easey, M. (2009). *Fashion Marketing*. Chichester, UK: John Wiley & Sons Ltd.

Gil-Or, O. (2010). Building consumer demand by using viral marketing tactics within an online social network. *Advances in Management*, 3(7), pp. 7–14.

Griffith, E. (2011). Bloggers Mean Business. *Ad Week* [online]. Available at: www.adweek.com/news/advertising-branding/bloggers-mean-business-134757 [accessed 10 August 2016].

Grunig, J.E. & Grunig, L.A. (2000). Public relations in strategic management and strategic management of public relations: Theory and evidence from the IABC Excellence project. *Journalism Studies*, 1(2), pp. 303–321.

Guzelis, G. (2010). *Characterising Successful Fashion Blogs and Their Evaluation Metrics*. Saarbrücken, Germany: LAP LAMBERT Academic Publishing.

Herzog, H. (1963). 'Behavioral Science Concepts for Analyzing the Consumer', in P. Bliss (ed.), *Marketing and the Behavioral Sciences*. Boston: Allyn and Bacon, Inc., pp. 76–86.

Hitt, M.A., Ireland, R.D. & Hoskisson, R.E. (2009). *Strategic management cases: Competitiveness and globalization*. Cengage Learning Hockerts.

Howells, R. (2011). Are You Ready for the Social Supply? *Forbes* [online]. Available from: www.forbes.com/sites/sap/2011/10/24/are-you-ready-for-the-socialsupply-chain/ [accessed 2 January 2017].

Kapferer, J.N. (1997). *Strategic Brand Management: Creating and Sustaining Brand Equity Long Term*, 2nd edn. London: Kogan Page Limited.

Kapferer, J.N. (2001). *Reinventing the Brand: Can Top Brands Survive the New Market Realities?* London: Kogan Page.

Kaplan, A.M. & Haenlein, M. (2010). Users of the world, unite! The challenges and opportunities of social media. *Business Horizons*, 53(1), pp. 59–68.

Knoll, M. & Bronstein, J. (2014). An examination of the information disclosure behavior of infertility bloggers. *Journal of Information Management*, 66(2), pp. 175–201.

Koubaa, Y. (2008). Country of origin, brand image perception, and brand image structure. *Asia Pacific Journal of Marketing and Logistics*, 20(2), pp. 139–155 [online]. Available at: www.emeraldinsight.com/doi/full/10.1108/13555850810864524 [accessed 18 April 2016].

Kozinets, R.V. (2006). *Netnography 2.0. Handbook of Qualitative Research Methods in Marketing*, ed. Russell W. Belk. Northampton, MA: Edward Elgar Publishing Inc, pp. 129–155.

Kretz, G. (2010). Pixelize Me!: A Semiotic Approach of Self-digitalization in Fashion Blogs. *Advances in Consumer Research*, 37. Duluth, MN: Association for Consumer Research.

Kuhn, M. (2007). Interactivity and Prioritizing the Human: A Code of Blogging Ethics. *Journal of Mass Media Ethics*, 22(1), pp. 18–36.

Lau, S. (2016). *Ikea: Swedish supply chain management machine*. Available from http://smbp. uwaterloo.ca/2015/10/ikea-swedish-supply-chain-management-machine/ [accessed 12 April 2016].

Lee, T.S., Leung, C.S. & Zhang, Z.M. (2009). Fashion Brand Image Marketing: Brand Image and Brand Personality. *RJTA*, 4(2), pp. 60–67.

Llamas, R. & Belk, W.R. (2013). *The Routledge Companion to Digital Consumption*. New York: Routledge.

Maehle, N. & Shneor, R. (2010). On congruence between brand and human personalities. *Journal of Product & Brand Management*, 19(1), pp. 44–53.

Malik, M. (2015). Value-enhancing capabilities of CSR: A brief review of contemporary literature. *Journal of Business Ethics*, 127(2), pp. 419–438.

Mangold, W.G. & Faulds, D.J. (2009). Social Media: The new hybrid element of the promotion mix. *Business Horizons*, 52, pp. 357–365.

Mohr, I. (2013). The Impact of Social Media on the Fashion Industry. *Journal of Applied Business and Economics*, 15(2).

Montpetit, H. (2015). GE embraces social media for supply chain management and business process improvement. Available from: http://smbp.uwaterloo.ca/2014/10/ge-embraces-socialmedia-for-supply-chain-management-and-business-process-improvement/ [accessed 12 March 2016].

Moore, C.M. & Docherty, A. (2007). 'The international flagship store of luxury fashion retailers', in T. Hines & M. Bruce (eds), *Fashion Marketing*. Oxford: Butterworth-Heinemann.

Mores, C.M. (2007). *From Fiorucci to the Guerrilla Stores: Shop Displays in Architecture, Marketing and Communications*. Oxford: Windsor Books.

Muniz, Jr.A.M. & O'Guinn, T.C. (2001). Brand Community. *Journal of Consumer Research*, 27(4), pp. 412–432.

Murugesan, S. (2007). Understanding Web 2.0. *IT Professional*, 9(4), pp. 34–41.

Nardi, B.A., Schiano, D.J., Gumbrecht, M. & Swartz, L. (2004). Why we blog. *Commun. ACM*, 47(12), pp. 41–46.

Nichols, M. (2010). Bloggers carry growing fashion industry influence. Reuters [online]. Available at: www.reuters.com/article/2010/09/15/us-newyork-fashion-internet-idUS TRE68E2II20100915 [accessed 10 August 2016].

Okazaki, S., Katsukura, A. & Nishiyama, M. (2007). How mobile advertising works: The role of trust in improving attitudes and recall. *Journal of Advertising Research*, 47(2), pp. 165–178.

O'Reilly, T. (2015). 'What is web 2.0', 30 September. Available at: Oreilly.com.

Ostberg, J. (2007). 'The linking value of subcultural capital: Constructing the Stockholm Brat enclave', in B. Cova, R.V. Kozinets & A. Shankar (eds), *Consumer Tribes*. Oxford: Elsevier/Butterworth-Heinemann, pp. 93–106.

Patterson, M. (1999). Re-Appraising the Concept of Brand Image. *Journal of Brand Management*, 6(6), pp. 409–426.

Patterson, P., Yu, T. & de Ruyter, K. (2006). Understanding customer engagement in services. *Advancing Theory, Maintaining Relevance, Proceedings of ANZMAC 2006 Conference, Brisbane* [online]. Available at: www.macs.hw.ac.uk/texturelab/files/publications/papers/ Papers_PDF/Perry_Digital_Tech_for_Textiles.pdf [accessed 18 April 2015].

Perry, J.L., Clough, P.J., Crust, L., Earle, K. & Nicholls, A.R. (2013). Factorial Validity of the Mental Toughness Questionnaire-48. *Personality and Individual Differences*, 54(5), pp. 587–592.

Piccione, M. & Rubinstein, A. (2008). Luxury prices, an expository note. *The Japanese Economic Review*, 59, pp. 127–132.

Prendergast, G., Phau, I. & Wong, C. (2000). 'An exploratory study of the purchase of luxury brands on infants apparel', in S. Chetty & B. Collins (eds), *Visionary Marketing for the 21st Century: Facing the Challenge: Proceedings 2000*. ANZMAC Conference, pp. 1005–1008.

Raeisi, S. & Lingjie, M. (2017). The Importance of Customer Engagement and Service Innovation in Value Co-Creation. *World Academy of Science, Engineering and Technology International Journal of Economics and Management Engineering*, 11(4).

Redsicker, P. (2013). Blogs Outrank Social Networks for Consumer Influence: New Research. *Social Media Examiner*, 6 March [online]. Available at: www.socialmediaexam iner.com/blogs-outrank-social-networks-for-consumer-influence-new-research/ [accessed 18 April 2016].

Reinach, S.S. (2005). China and Italy: Fast fashion versus prêt a porter – towards a new culture of fashion. *Fashion Theory*, 9(1), pp. 43–56.

Schau, H.J. & Gilly, M.C. (2003). We are What We Post? Self-presentation in Personal Web Space. *Journal of Consumer Research*, 30(3), p. 385.

Sedeke, K. (2012). *Effective Fashion Blogs and Their Impact on the Current Fashion Industry* [online]. Available at: Users/abc/Downloads/Sedeke.pdf [accessed 10 December 2016].

Shao, G. (2008). Understanding the appeal of user-generated media: A uses and gratification perspective. *Internet Research*, 19(1), pp. 7–25.

Sika, V. (2014). *Fashion for Feminists: How Fashion and Dress Shape Women's Identities*. Available in: www.osisa.org/buwa/regional/fashion-feministshow-fashion-and-dress-shape-women-identities/http [accessed December 2017].

Smith, K.T. (2011). Digital marketing strategies that millennials find appealing, motivating, or just annoying. *Journal of Strategic Marketing*, 19(6), pp. 489–499.

Taylor, L. (2015). Past, present and future: Social media creates dramatic changes for DQ supply chain. Available from: http://smbp.uwaterloo.ca/2015/10/past-present-and-future-social-mediacreates-dramatic-changes-for-dq-supply-chain/ [accessed 17 February 2017].

THREAD (2009). *Seeds of Hunger: Intellectual property rights on seeds and the human rights response*. Backgrounder 2 in the THREAD series. Available at: www.3dthree.org/pdf_3D/3D_THREAD2seeds.pdf [accessed December 2017].

Tokatli, N. (2007). Global sourcing: Insights from the global clothing industry – the case of Zara, a fast fashion retailer. *Journal of Economic Geography*, 8, pp. 21–38.

Wang, Q. (2011). Autobiographical Memory and Culture. *Online Readings in Psychology and Culture*, 5(2).

Wattanasuwan, K. (2005). The self and symbolic consumption. *Journal of American Academy of Business* [online]. Available at: file:///Users/abc/Downloads/Wattanasuwan.pdf [accessed 18 April 2016].

Wei, L. (2009). Filter blogs vs. personal journals: Understanding the knowledge production gap on the Internet. *Journal of Computer-Mediated Communication*, 14(3), pp. 532–558.

Williams, D.L. et al. (2012). The use of social media: An exploratory study of uses among digital natives. *Journal of Public Affairs*, 12(2), pp. 127–136.

Woodside, A., Sood, S. & Miller, K. (2008). When Consumers and Brands Talk: Story-telling Theory and Research in Psychology and Marketing. *Psychology and Marketing*, 25 (2), pp. 97–145.

Workman, J.E. (2010). Fashion consumer groups, gender, and need for touch. *Clothing and Textiles Research Journal*, 28, pp. 126–139.

Zhao, X. & Belk, R.W. (2007). 'Live from Shopping Malls: Blogs and Chinese Consumer Desire', in G. Fitzsimons & V. Morwitz, *Advances in Consumer Research*, vol. 34. Valdosta, GA: Association of Consumer Research.

9

THE GLOBAL SUPPLY CHAIN RISK MANAGEMENT

9.1 Introduction

Over the last decades, huge amounts of multinational enterprises have confronted great challenges operating in the global supply chain networks. It has been pointed out that the danger of the global supply chain has been increasing and the network has become more complex since the financial crisis in 2008 (*Financial Times*, 2016). More specifically, currency fluctuations in the foreign market are able to cause excess inventory with eroded margins, and legal issues can result in financial losses and negative effects on reputation for multinational firms. Primark, for example, has paid compensation of millions of pounds due to the collapse of a poorly constructed building in Bangladesh that killed over 1,100 people (*Financial Times*, 2016). Therefore, the underlying risks within the global supply chain are essential to be managed and mitigated, and effective and efficient global supply chain risk management (SCRM) has become an important objective for global decision makers.

9.2 Supply chain risk

Supply chain risk management is defined as 'events are characterized by the probability of occurrence and their related consequences' (Heckmann et al., 2015, p.121). To be specific, Wieland and Wallenburg (2012) define it as the implementation of strategies for daily and exceptional risks management within the global supply chain in order to mitigate vulnerability and achieve sustainability.

It is believed that proactive risk management enables decision makers to prevent failure, mitigate effects of failure and recover from the effects of failure. Much existing literature suggests various approaches to measure and reduce risks in the global supply chain using different models such as a decision analysis approach

(Berger et al., 2004), stochastic model (Goh et al., 2007), and quantitative method (Heckmann et al., 2015). The main purpose of this chapter is to identify various risks in the global supply chain and propose one solution to manage these risks for global decision makers with critical analysis.

With the evolution of the global market, global supply chains have become more interrelated and complex. Manuj and Mentzer (2008) state that although it is difficult to manage the complex global supply chain, the majority of multinational enterprises are still pursuing opportunity in the global market because of the cheap labour and raw materials cost, subsidised financing opportunities, greater product market and various inducements by different regulations. However, global companies confront the fact that the underlying risks and uncertainties in the global supply chain could cause widespread disruption. According to Hendricks and Singhal (2005), between 1989 and 2000, more than 800 supply chain disruptions occurred and firms faced decreasing sales by 93%, a decline in operating income by 107%, diminishing returns on assets by 114%, lower shareholder returns by 33% to 40%, and higher share price volatility by 13.5%. Moreover, based on the study by Ben Hamida and Gugler (2008), it illustrates the subsequent consequences caused by the supply chain risk (*The Economist*, 2006).

In order to reduce the risk and provide an approach to risk management in the global supply market, the five-step risk-based method has been applied to mitigate risks step by step. This easily constructed integrated framework is regarded as a proactive method of a step-by-step model and enables decision makers to understand different types of risk in a straightforward process. It also combines qualitative and quantitative risks in the framework, thereby providing different aspects of risk analysis.

It provides the operation of the supply chain in the dynamic environment, in which it allows decision makers to react promptly with updated risk data and information in changes of environments and organisations. Nevertheless, there are limitations to this framework. Specifically, a forecast error in the early steps would incur the inaccuracy of the whole process due to the correlation of each step. Secondly, since the framework is integrated and complex, it is time consuming and unmanageable. Moreover, this approach is potentially not adjusted into every risk management case. Furthermore, this framework fails to show the relationship with performance of the supply chain and there are still massive elements that need to be concerned. Therefore, it is important for decision makers to be cautious of estimation, flexible in different risk management cases, inserting more quantitative instruments and monitoring the process to implement and moderate the framework in the global supply chain integrated risk management to mitigate the underlying risk.

9.3 Global supply chain risk

In order to understand supply chain risk, it is defined as 'the probability of occurrence of disruptive events' (Heckmann et al., 2015). Risks in the supply chain are

106 Global supply chain risk management

divided into sources and types of risks (Svensson, 2000, 2002), and also can be categorised as quantitative risks such as financial loss and qualitative risks such as losing reliability (Manuj & Mentzer, 2008). Jüttner et al. (2003) divide risk sources into environmental risk, organisational risk and network-related risk. Similarly, Deleris and Erhun (2007) identify different supply chain risk types more specifically as operational (forecast errors, transportation risks, etc.), social (labour shortages, human and organisational errors, etc.), natural disaster (fire, flood, earthquake, etc.), economy (interest rate fluctuation, exchange rate fluctuation, etc.), and political (lawsuits, governmental restriction, etc.).

The existing literature gives similar definitions of global SCRM. Norrman and Jansson (2004) state risk management as the process of risk acceptance and implementation of actions to mitigate the consequences, while Narasimhan and Talluri (2009) consider it strategic management with the impacts of risks on operational and financial performance in the company. Moreover, Heckmann et al. (2015) illustrate that the concept of 'resilience' is applied in crisis and emergency management to respond to threat, and supply chain resilience has been developed as the ability to mitigate supply chain risks.

Nevertheless, it has been indicated that it is hard to manage the risks' consequences and firms could be influenced by critical incidents easily (Harland et al., 2003). With regard to the report by UPS Capital (Dittmann, 2014), 90% of decision makers neglect SCRM and over 60% of firms are under low effective management. The majority of existing research applies tactical processes to approach SCRM as risk identification, risk assessment and evaluation, selection of appropriate risk management, implementation of SCRM strategy and mitigation of supply chain risks (Norrman & Jansson, 2004; Manuj & Mentzer, 2008; Zhao & Huchzermeier, 2015), which is used as the solution to global supply chain risk management.

9.4 Importance of supply chain risk management

The powerful 2016 Kumamoto earthquakes forced major players such as Toyota, Honda, Nissan and Sony to suspend their production across various sites in Japan. The disruption was contributed by a mixture of supply disruption, primarily the sensor supplies, and damage to the production factories (*Fortune*, 2016). Highly complex and inter-contingent global supply chains and a dearth of visibility of the sub-suppliers are some of the critical factors influencing the recovery timescales. A study by the supply chain firm Resilinc revealed that around 800 industrial facilities including factories, distribution centres, warehouses, etc., were affected in the region of Texas (MH&L, 2017).

In 2017, six countries including the United Arab Emirates, Saudi Arabia and Bahrain instantaneously retrenched all political and business traffic with Qatar, indicting the state for financing terrorism. As the country utterly relies on imports, the abrupt shutdown of its land, air and sea borders by its neighbouring nations rapidly affected its supply chain even leading people to panic purchase in supermarkets contemplating the possibility of shortages (CIPS, 2017).

According to Ritchie and Brindley (2007), supply chain disruptions affect supply chain performance which in turn influences business profitability. Different supply chain issues bring about varying impacts to organisations' operational performance. It was observed that the stock value and financial bottom line of organisations were adversely affected by supply chain disruptions and issues from a large sample research (Hendricks & Singhal, 2005). Prolonged lead times, material shortages, failing customer orders and rising operational costs are a few key characteristic ramifications of supply chain disruptions (Riddalls & Bennett, 2002; Chopra & Sodhi, 2004).

Consulting firm CapGemini and KRC Research surveyed supply chain managers across the world and found that 54% reported that supply chain disruptions and issues had had an adverse effect on their organisation's financial performance in the past few years (CapGemini, 2013). Diageo, a global manufacturer and distributor of premium alcoholic beverages, declared that they customised their distribution strategy, integrated risk mitigation to their business model and segmented their product portfolio and its supply chains to minimise the impact of supply chain disruptions in Asia (*Supply Chain Quarterly*, 2018).

Starbucks Coffee Co., one of the global beverage companies, has entrenched an enterprise-wide risk management programme to determine developing trends that could disrupt its supply chain and impede its customer service operations (*Supply Chain Quarterly*, 2014). The global supply chain institute at the University of Tennessee deduced that organisations that focused on cost cutting often failed to spot various potential risks ingrained in their complex supply chains in their research. A number of organisations precipitated into globalisation with indefensible optimism and have learnt hard lessons (*Supply Chain Quarterly*, 2015).

In a survey conducted by the World Economic Forum, over 90% of the respondents indicated that SCRM has gained precedence in their respective organisations over the past five years (World Economic Forum, 2012). Consequently, the management of the supply chain in today's competitive world is gaining ground rapidly amongst managers and supply chain professionals because of the inimical effects that these supply chain issues can have on organisational performance. All the above scenarios perspicuously demonstrate the importance of supply chain risk management in an organisation. An organisation's SCRM framework heavily governs the future of its supply chain.

9.5 Risk drivers

Competitive factors and trends that are imperative for an organisation to enhance efficiency and market competitiveness are termed the risk drivers. According to Jüttner, Peck and Christopher (2003), it is vital for organisations to identify risk drivers of one's own operational supply chain as these are highly inclined to increase the vulnerability of the organisation. Some examples may include a condensed product cycle, single source of supply, long-distance logistics, globally scattered supplier locations, complex product and process designs, etc. In fact, the supply chain framework and the associated practices themselves might well be a risk driver (Jüttner, 2005). Global dispersal of the supply chain undoubtedly generates access to low-cost workforce, cost-effective raw materials and wide-ranging marketplace; nonetheless it results in fluctuating and prolonged lead times thereby resulting in delivery uncertainty (Norrman & Lindroth, 2004).

Various cardinal risk drivers were identified by Ritchie and Brindley (2007) and were classified as strategic, tactical and operational. The strategic drivers include technology development, innovative product development, shorter product life cycle, etc., whereas tactical drivers are mainly associated with supply chain interactions, a few being linked with sales performance, training and development needs, and logistics performance.

The operational drivers are predominantly related to robust stock management, streamlined sales order processing, etc. (Zsidisin et al., 2005). Organisations that pursue improvement in their efficiency by reducing their operational costs and supplying a wider marketplace are coerced to have a substantial network in which the likelihood of risks and disruptions is directly proportional (Zsidisin & Wagner, 2010). The propagation of risks or disruptions throughout the entire supply chain is a critical failure mode in these types of interconnected and complex supply chains. Therefore, it is vital that the business managers and supply chain professionals consider these risks during their decision-making process to balance operational efficiency and supply chain robustness (Hayes et al., 2005).

In recent times, the emerging trend of a lean supply chain also poses risks to an organisation's supply chain. According to Hauser (2003), and Wagner and Bode (2006), the more dependent as well as leaner the supply chains are, the higher the probability of disruptions at any node of the supply chain. Another risk driver identified from the literature search is business process outsourcing (BPO). Despite BPO claims to lower operational risks, the lack of control over the outsourced processes tends to elevate the risk exposure for an organisation (Kotabe et al., 2008).

Various studies have broadly categorised the enablers as proactive and reactive risk management strategies (Kilubi & Haasis, 2015; Manuj et al., 2014; Wieland & Wallenburg, 2012; Thun & Hoenig, 2011). In a study conducted by Thun and Hoenig (2011), it was observed that the organisations adopting proactive strategies demonstrate rapid response, improved flexibility and stock reduction, while the companies following reactive methods exhibit reduction of the bullwhip effect they were experiencing in the past. Hence, by amalgamating the two strategies, an organisation can draw on the benefits of both methods.

Various authors acknowledge the vitality of data collection and its usage in the planning process as it augments the organisation's capabilities to manage supply chain risks (Fawcett et al., 2011). Besides enabling the establishment of eventuality planning, information transparency and visibility play a critical role to manage day-to-day operations. The information sharing with the supply chain partners is as significant as sharing it within the organisation, thereby leading to faster decision making, an increased supply chain response rate, and a coordinated and improved supply chain performance (Sanders & Premus, 2005).

9.6 Five-step integrated risk management framework

To address the solution of global supply chain risk management, the general approach is presented as a five-step process for integrated risk management. The following shows this approach to solving global supply chain risk management.

Initially, in step one, decision makers distinguish different types of risks that are potentially occurring in both domestic and global markets, as well as identifying previous failure modes (Layzell & Ledbetter, 1998), which enables decision makers to create a risks profile (Manuj & Mentzer, 2008) for screening and categorising different uncertainties (Zhao & Huchzermeier, 2015).

Second of all, risks require assessment and evaluation by decision makers. In other words, it is to quantify and prioritise the causes of failure based on likelihood.

Thirdly, decision makers select appropriate strategies to manage risks, which is to develop the risk mitigation plans and develop improvement, for example implementing a cost-benefit analysis (Ben Hamida and Gugler, 2008). Moreover, this is regarded as the selection of operational hedging and financial flexibility (Zhao & Huchzermeier, 2015). Specifically, Zhao and Huchzermeier (2015) classify the hedging strategies into six flexibilities: supply (multi-sourcing, backup supply, etc.); processing (production flexibility, modularisation, etc.); demand (demand shifting, allocation options, etc.); network (supply chain network options, network configuration, etc.); time (advance and postponement flexibility); and a mix of the preceding five elements. Furthermore, Zhao and Huchzermeier (2015) outline three instruments for financial flexibility, referring to the quantifying risks, which are cash instrument, supply chain instrument and derivative instrument.

Step four is implementing risk management strategies with the trends of globalisation and growing customised product offerings. Freedman (2003) indicates the key objective in this step is to reduce complexity, and it is critical to obtain the most important information by filtering the data. In the final step, supply chain risk management requires mitigation and monitoring in case the unexpected event occurs and it also maintains the plan with a quick response to changes (Grammich, 2011).

This five-step global supply chain risk management process provides the framework of integrated risk management and enables global decision makers to identify, evaluate, manage and mitigate risks. It also provides a straightforward framework which allows decision makers to view all important elements of the problem. This framework is simple and transparent to construct and it is customised for different situations. Manuj and Mentzer (2008) identify three advantages of this framework for global supply chain risk management. First of all, global supply chain risk decisions are managed by a step-by-step model for decision makers to shift the typical intuitive thinking towards proactive risk management. For example, it helps decision makers to comprehend different types of risks and use the risk profile to implement appropriate strategies in the global market. Secondly, this framework takes qualitative and quantitative risks into consideration by using multiple risk assessment tools. Thirdly, it explicitly shows the operation of a supply chain in the dynamic environment. Given this, it is able to adopt different strategies as a continuous guideline when changes to the environment and organisation incur uncertainties because of updated and useful risk data and information.

On the other hand, there are several disadvantages to this framework. Initially, as the framework is a step-by-step approach and every step is correlated with each other, any forecast error or wrong estimation in previous steps would cause the inaccuracy of the following process. Secondly, with huge, complex decisions, this five-step approach could be time consuming and unmanageable. Thirdly, risk management is broad, and the risk in the research could be not applied in one company as it is not specific.

Moreover, Ben Hamida and Gugler (2008) argue that the historical and perceived behaviours by customers require decision makers to proactively estimate any fluctuation in the market; however, it is still hard to forecast due to the greater uncertainty in the market. Furthermore, the framework addresses the mitigation of the global supply chain throughout large amounts of elements while the risk could be rising due to the inaccuracy of estimation by human error. On the other hand, this framework fails to show the relationship with supply chain performance (Manuj & Mentzer, 2008). Although it provides different tools of risk assessment during the process and combines qualitative and quantitative risks, here it merely shows the general process for global supply chain risk management. There are still massive elements and details requiring consideration.

Referring to improvement of this solution, in order to eliminate underlying risks in this framework because of the correlation of each step, it is significant for decision makers to make decisions and implement strategies precisely during the process. Moreover, simulate the integrated framework with various experiments, summarise failures and improve them to avoid those mistakes. Computing science is also able to avoid underlying risks caused by human error and also solve the time consuming and unmanageable nature of this integrated framework.

Manuj and Mentzer (2008) suggest future research on the relationship with integrated global supply chain risk management framework and supply chain performance, and the measurement of performance should be realistic, representative, consistent, cost effective, understandable, as well as not underdetermined (Mentzer & Firman, 1994). Decision makers also need to be flexible with different risk management cases and avoid wrongly applying the framework to every different company, which should be implemented case by case. Finally, Heckmann et al. (2015) indicate the standard deviation, mean variance approaches to measure risk for decision makers, which provide detailed quantitative instruments in risk assessment for global supply chain risk management and enable decision makers to obtain more information of risk measurement and take more elements into consideration. As a consequence, the moderate implementation of the framework, precise analysis and cautious monitoring would lead decision makers to mitigate global supply chain risk.

9.7 Summary

The rapid development of globalisation over the last decades has led multinational firms to pursue cross-border business activities. The global supply chains have been integrated and become more complex. The uncertainties, dynamics and accidents in one link tend to more likely influence other links in the network with the increasing integrated supply chain. Moreover, it is believed that the damage to the global supply chain has increased since the financial crisis in 2008 and the majority of firms have confronted the negative consequences due to the destroyed global supply chain. Therefore, it is significant for decision makers to be aware of underlying risks in the global supply chain and mitigate these risks with appropriate risk management.

This chapter has outlined that the risk in the global supply chain can cause widespread disruption such as loss of sales, profits and market share. Risk can be classified as quantitative and qualitative risk, and is also divided into different types of risk such as operational, social, economy, political and natural disaster. Schmidt and Wilhelm (2000) indicate that it is essential for global supply chains to consider distinctions in economies, politics, culture and competitive markets. Additionally, global supply chain risk management is also a problem for decision makers when global supply chain risk occurs. It is considered as strategies and process to implement actions for risk mitigation. Surprisingly, there exist some companies unaware of the method of supply chain risk management.

References

Basu, G., Benhamida, M., Butner, K. et al. (2007). *Supply Chain Risk Management: A Delicate Balancing Act.* IBM Corporation.

Ben Hamida, L. & Gugler, P. (2008). 'FDI and spillovers in the Swiss manufacturing industry: Interaction effects between spillover mechanisms and domestic absorptive capacities', in Maryann P. Feldman & Grazia D. Santangelo (eds), *New Perspectives in International Business Research.* Progress in International Business Research, Vol. 3. Emerald Group Publishing Ltd, pp. 263–287.

Berger, Paul D., Gerstenfeld, Arther & Zeng, Amy Z. (2004). How Many Suppliers are Best? A Decision-analysis Approach. *Omega (Oxford)*, 32(1), pp. 9–15.

CapGemini (2013). *The Supply Chain Impact Survey* (ebook), p. 10. Available at: www.capgemini.com/wpcontent/uploads/2017/07/capgemini_scm_and_consumer_survey.pdf [accessed 15 February 2018].

Chopra, S. & Sodhi, M. (2004). Managing risk to avoid supply-chain breakdown. *MIT Sloan Management Review*, 46(1), pp. 53–61.

CIPS (2017). Qatar's supply chains 'instantly disrupted' [online]. Available at: www.cips.org/supply-management/news/2017/june/qatars-supply-chains-instantly-disrupted-/ [accessed 22 October 2017].

Deleris, L.A. & Erhun, F. (2007). 'Risk Management in a Supply Network: A Case Study Based on Engineering Risk Analysis Concepts', in K. Kempf, P. Keskinocak & R. Uzsoy (eds), *Handbook of Production Planning.* Kluwer International Series in Operations Research and Management Science, Kluwer Academic Publishers.

Dittmann, J. Paul (2014). *Managing Risk in the Global Supply Chain*. UPS Capital Corporation [online]. Available at: https://upscapital.com/wp-content/themes/upscapital-bren/assets/media/Managing-Risk-in-the-Global-Supply-Chain-ebook.pdf [accessed 16 April 2017].

The Economist (2006). When the chain breaks [online]. Available at: www.economist.com/node/7032258 [accessed 16 April 2017].

Fawcett, S.E., Wallin, C., Allred, C., Fawcett, A.M. & Magnan, G.M. (2011). Information technology as an enabler of supply chain collaboration: A dynamic capabilities perspective. *Journal of Supply Chain Management*, 47(1), pp. 38–56.

Financial Times (2013). Global supply chains face heightened risks [online]. Available at: www.ft.com/content/09e05786-f6f6-11e4-99aa-00144feab7de [accessed 16 April 2017].

Financial Times (2016). Complex supply chains spell trouble for companies trying to manage risk [online]. Available at: www.ft.com/content/2cf5bebe-9773-11e5-9228-87e603d47bdc [accessed 16 April 2017].

Fortune (2016). Kumamoto Quake Shakes Up Toyota's Supply Chain [online]. Available at: http://fortune.com/2016/04/17/toyota-earthquake-disruptions/ [accessed 11 October 2017].

Freedman, Mike (2003). The Genius is in the Implementation. *Journal of Business Research*, 24 (2), pp. 26–31.

Goh, M., Lim. J. & Meng, F. (2007). A stochastic model for risk management in global supply chain networks. *European Journal of Operational Research*, 182, pp. 164–173.

Grammich, C. (2011). *Supply Chain Risk Management: A Compilation of Best Practices*. [accessed 15 April 2017].

Harland, Christine, Brenchley, Richard & Walker, Helen (2003). Risk in Supply Networks. *Journal of Purchasing and Supply Management*, 9(2), pp. 51–62.

Hauser, L. (2003). Risk adjusted supply chain management. *Supply Chain Management Review*, 7(6), pp. 64–71.

Hayes, R., Pisano, G., Upton, D. & Wheelwright, S. (2005). *Operations, Strategy, and Technology: Pursuing the Competitive Edge*. Hoboken, NJ: Wiley.

Heckmann, I., Comes, T. & Nickel, S. (2015). A critical review on supply chain risk: Definition, measure and modelling. *Omega*, 52 (April), pp. 119–132.

Hendricks, K. & Singhal, V. (2005). An empirical analysis of the effect of supply chain disruptions on long run stock price performance and equity risk of the firm. *Production and Operations Management*, 14(1), pp. 35–52.

Hendricks, K.B. & Singhal, V.R. (2012). 'Supply Chain Disruptions and Corporate Performance', in H. Gurnani, A. Mehrotra & S. Ray (ed.), *Supply Chain Disruptions: Theory and Practice of Managing Risk*. London: Springer Verlag London Ltd.

Jüttner, U. (2005). Supply chain risk management: Understanding the business requirements from a practitioner perspective. *The International Journal of Logistics Management*, 16(1), pp. 120–141.

Jüttner, U., Peck, H. & Christopher, M. (2003). Supply Chain Risk Management: Outlining an Agenda for Future Research. *International Journal of Logistics: Research & Applications*, 6(4), pp. 197–210.

Kilubi, I. & Haasis, H. (2015). Supply Chain Risk Management Enablers: A Framework Development Through Systematic Review of the Literature from 2000 to 2015. *International Journal of Business Science & Applied Management*, 10(1), pp. 35–54.

Kotabe, M., Riege, A., Griffiths, K., Noble, G., Ang, S.H., Pecotich, A. & Helsen, K. (2008). *International Marketing*, 2nd Asia-Pacific edn. Wiley.

Layzell, J. & Ledbetter, S. (1998). FMEA applied to cladding systems reducing the risk of failure. *Building Research and Information*, 26(6), pp. 351–357.

Manuj, I., Esper, T. & Stank, T. (2014). Supply Chain Risk Management Approaches Under Different Conditions of Risk. *Journal of Business Logistics*, 35(3), pp. 241–258.

Manuj, I. & Mentzer, John T. (2008). Global Supply Chain Risk Management. *Journal of Business Logistics*, 29(1), p. 133.

Mentzer, John T. & Firman, John (1994). Logistics Control Systems in the 21st Century. *Journal of Business Logistics*, 15(1), pp. 215–227.

MH&L (2017). Supply Chain Impact of Hurricane Harvey Could Be Worse than Expected. *Material Handling and Logistics (MHL News)* [online]. Available at: www.mhlnews.com/global-supply-chain/supply-chain-impact-hurricane-harvey-could-be-worse-expected [accessed 15 October 2017].

Narasimhan, R. & Talluri, S. (2009). Special Issue: Perspectives on Risk Management in Supply Chains. *Journal of Operations Management*, 27(2), pp. 114–118.

Norrman, A. & Jansson, U. (2004). Ericsson's proactive supply chain risk management approach after a serious sub-supplier accident. *International Journal of Physical Distribution & Logistics Management*, 34(5), pp. 434–456.

Norrman, A. & Lindroth, R. (2004). Categorization of supply chain risk and risk management. *Supply Chain Risk*, pp. 14–27.

Riddalls, C. & Bennett, S. (2002). Production–inventory system controller design and supply chain dynamics. *International Journal of Systems Science*, 33(3), pp. 181–195.

Ritchie, B. & Brindley, C. (2007). Supply chain risk management and performance: A guiding framework for future development. *International Journal of Operations & Production Management*, 27(3), pp. 303–322.

Sanders, N. & Premus, R. (2005). Modeling the relationship between firm it capability, collaboration, and performance. *Journal of Business Logistics*, 26(1), pp. 1–23.

Schmidt, G. & Wilbert, E. Wilhelm (2000). Strategic, Tactical and Operational Decisions in Multi-National Logistics Networks: A Review and Discussion of Modelling Issues. *International Journal of Production Research*, 38(7), pp. 1501–1523.

Supply Chain Quarterly (2014). Starbucks adds risk management program to help protect its supply chain. *CSCMP's Supply Chain Quarterly* [online]. Available at: www.supplychainquarterly.com/news/20140226-starbucks-adds-risk-management-program-to-help-protect-its-supply-chain/ [accessed 2 February 2018].

Supply Chain Quarterly (2015). Two approaches to mitigating supply chain risk. *CSCMP's Supply Chain Quarterly* [online]. Available at: www.supplychainquarterly.com/columns/20150331-two-approaches-to-mitigating-supply-chain-risk/ [accessed 18 February 2018].

Supply Chain Quarterly (2018). How Diageo reduced risk in Asia – strategy. *CSCMP's Supply Chain Quarterly* [online]. Available at: www.supplychainquarterly.com/topics/strategy/20140613-how-diageo-reduced-risk-in-asia/ [accessed 16 February 2018].

Svensson, G. (2000). A conceptual framework for the analysis of vulnerability in supply chains. *International Journal of Physical Distribution & Logistics Management*, 30(9), pp. 731–750.

Svensson, G. (2002). A conceptual framework of vulnerability in firms' inbound and outbound logistics flows. *International Journal of Physical Distribution & Logistics Management*, 32(2), pp. 110–134.

Thun, J. & Hoenig, D. (2011). An empirical analysis of supply chain risk management in the German automotive industry. *International Journal of Production Economics*, 131(1), pp. 242–249.

Wagner, S. & Bode, C. (2006). An empirical investigation into supply chain vulnerability. *Journal of Purchasing and Supply Management*, 12(6), pp. 301–312.

Wieland, A. & Marcus Wallenburg, C. (2012). Dealing with supply chain risks: Linking risk management practices and strategies to performance. *International Journal of Physical Distribution & Logistics Management*, 42(10), pp. 887–905, doi: doi:10.1108/09600031211281411.

World Economic Forum (2012). *New Models for Addressing Supply Chain and Transport Risk*. Geneva: World Economic Forum.

Zhao, L. & Huchzermeier, A. (2015). Operations – finance interface models: A literature review and framework. *European Journal of Operational Research*, 244, pp. 905–917.

Zsidisin, G., Melnyk, S. & Ragatz, G. (2005). An institutional theory perspective of business continuity planning for purchasing and supply management. *International Journal of Production Research*, 43(16), pp. 3401–3420.

Zsidisin, G. & Wagner, S. (2010). Do perceptions become reality? The moderating role of supply chain resiliency on disruption occurrence. *Journal of Business Logistics*, 31(2), pp. 1–20.

10

A DELIVERY SYSTEM FOR SAINSBURY'S CLOTHING BRAND

10.1 Introduction

The UK's famous supermarket Sainsbury's has taken its own clothing brand Tu from a standing start in 2004 to record sales of £680 million in 2012 (*Kirklees Business News*, 2013, p.2).[1] In the first season of 2014, Tu performed well continually, despite the supermarket reporting a decrease in total sales of 1.5% for ten weeks to 15 March 2014 (Neilan, 2014). In early 2015, Sainsbury's was expected to open a new 1 million square foot distribution centre at Daventry International rail freight terminal to face possible delivery issues (Brooks, 2013). Tu was chosen as a case study to state how to deal with the problem of lack of delivery of Tu clothing to the nearest store or a customer's home by online shopping, which may reduce customers' experience and the efficiency of Sainsbury's business. The focus will be on the delivery system for Tu and what methods will be adopted for outcomes, which will be discussed further below.

Delivery is one of the situational factors affecting consumers' decisions of whether to shop online (Huang & Oppewal, 2006). There are four factors: delivery charge, time availability, travel time to the store, and trip purpose influencing the choice of delivery. One of the delivery methods is click and collect. With click and collect, consumers can order online, and collect their items at the pick-up point (Fernie et al., 2003; Durand & Senkel, 2007). This has proven itself to be a key success for major grocery 'bricks and mortar' retailers in their development of the click and collect approach. The click and collect model is gaining increasing support and making a particular contribution to the development of the internet channel and online ordering. There are two models, the first 'attached' to an existing store, the second one a 'solo' outlet, which correspond to different strategic objectives: the first is defensive, the second more aggressive in terms of the competition (Nielsen, 2011). Many large French grocery retailers are investing

116 Case study: an apparel delivery system

heavily in click and collect formats in order to avoid having to make home deliveries and bear the substantial costs associated with the 'last mile', but they still have to deal with a new and difficult format (Colla & Lapoule, 2012).

10.2 Problem identification

The problem that has been identified is that Sainsbury's has no delivery system in place which will allow customers' online orders from Tu to be delivered. The problem was found after researching Sainsbury's and what they are lacking in comparison to competitors. Sainsbury's main competitor is Tesco F&F, who have a competitive advantage over Sainsbury's as they have a delivery system in place for online shopping with their clothing range. Looking at profits and sales, Tesco's F&F range has been successful, exhibited in their online growth of 13%, which has taken group sales above £3 billion (Neilan, 2013). Contrastingly, Sainsbury's only has a 7% rise (Davey, 2013).

There are many other issues surrounding the initial problem of the lack of delivery systems in place for online orders of Sainsbury's Tu range. Firstly, with the delivery of online orders there will be extra costs for the customer and the retailer, which could be an issue for both parties especially the consumer as they may not be willing to spend more money for delivery. According to Dr Clive Black, delivery fees may arise due to the increase in online shoppers (Bryant et al., 2012). The costs of deliveries could vary depending on whether Sainsbury's chooses to use a third party to make the deliveries. If Sainsbury's does not choose to use a third party they will need to invest more time and money in creating their own service.

Having to meet customer delivery windows and nominated days adds complexity and inefficiency to the operation (Browne & Gomez, 2011). The order will need to travel from the depot to the customer within the allocated window; however, this could collide with the depot working hours, traffic, and weather conditions and parking restrictions in urban areas. Vehicle routing and scheduling is the actual application used in transportation planning and consists of assigning loads/customers to the available fleet of vehicles and schedule these vehicles to follow the optimum routes so the cost of the operation is minimised (Browne & Gomez, 2011). This could potentially be another issue because it may collide with customer delivery windows, because the customer's desired delivery time may not be the same as what is available in that area.

There are additionally going to be delivery difficulties in both urban and suburban areas. This is more common in urban areas as specific urban policies also have an impact on the urban logistics distribution, making it more complex and costly (Browne & Gomez 2011). For example, speed limits, parking regulations and bus lanes all have an impact as they could make the initial delivery route longer which is likely to increase costs and time.

Sainsbury's will need to make sure all drivers have been trained to stick to the urban policies as it will be very costly to Sainsbury's if the drivers do not follow urban policies. Another impact of transportation within an urban area is on the environment, air quality, safety, noise pollution and congestion. With this being said, the logistics and transport industry are under pressure to 'green' their operations and become more efficient (Browne & Gomez 2011). Suburban areas will have similar issues; however, the main issue will be delivery time windows for customers. In suburban areas residents are more likely to be living farther apart which will add more time and costs to the delivery schedule.

When implementing this delivery system another issue that will need to be addressed is the flow of goods from the supplier all the way to the consumer. As Sainsbury's are currently using a system that doesn't involve delivery of non-grocery items, this could mean that Sainsbury's distribution centres may not be able to facilitate these new goods as well as the new delivery system as they may not have the resources to do so. Sainsbury's will further need to think how the goods are going to get from the supplier to the distribution centre, to the depot and then to the customer, and how lengthy the process of delivery will be.

All in all, it has been clarified that there are many issues surrounding the initial problem which is that Sainsbury's has no delivery system in place to allow the customer to order online from their Tu range and have it delivered. The main issues will be the flow of goods from supplier to consumer, vehicle routing and scheduling, and complying with rules and regulations of urban areas. Once these issues are resolved and solutions are found, Sainsbury's will be able to implement a time- and cost-efficient delivery system for their Tu range online that will benefit both Sainsbury's and the consumer.

10.3 Home delivery

Home delivery is where the product is delivered directly from the retailer's warehouse to a customer's home. It is a common delivery type in contemporary society. Most retailers provide this kind of service with their own delivery system or outsource to a third-party delivery company. Several different kinds of delivery concepts and service levels are being provided to make it consummate, like the delivery time window, which is how long a customer should stay at home and wait.

First of all, home delivery can serve a much wider customer base. As it is known, home delivery is closely related to online shopping. Wherever the shop is and whatever the product is being sold, by the means of delivery, it is easy to send products to customers. Home delivery can serve different age groups of people. On the other hand, home delivery can look forward to customer retention and help the brand or the company gain more customers. It can also be time saving for some consumers and also for some retailers, i.e. Sainsbury's has areas with large distribution centres like Thameside, so surrounding areas may be fairly easy and low cost to deliver to. 'Home delivery offers an important way for companies to reconnect with the busy and stressed out customers' (Boyer, 2003, p.662). These kinds of consumers do not have time to purchase and collect items via in-store delivery, and by offering this service they again give themselves direct competition with other retailers.

118 Case study: an apparel delivery system

Secondly, 'home delivery helps customers reduce impulse and unnecessary purchases' (Boyer, 2003, p.654). Sometimes impulse buys are good for the development of stores, but do not satisfy customers. To some extent, impulse purchases may reduce the desire of customers to buy the product and the retailers may lose some potential customers. Boyer et al. (2003) conclude that home delivery is an excellent value-added service for the segment of market. It places a premium on convenience over low price, which encourages customers to buy more products.

First of all, home delivery can be time consuming and inefficient. Products that are purchased online have to be picked out one by one and packaged, then sent to the delivery station to deliver to each customer. This kind of slow picking can be a big problem of home delivery. Punakivi and Saranen (2001) identified that inefficient home delivery increases operational costs in the e-grocery business. The cost of home delivery transportation service is closely related to the amount of vans being used in the delivery part, as well as the number of vans needed during the same time window. As for home delivery, customers have the ability to choose a delivery time. In doing so, customers are able to control the home delivery time window and service, which could make the cost higher.

A larger amount of staff are needed for the delivery including those working at distribution centres, customer services and perhaps those delivering the items, depending on whether the brand uses a courier or their own drivers. Companies have to consider not only the salary paid to these staff but also a waste of human resources. As mentioned before, customers choose the delivery time, which can lead to longer working hours for the staff. If there are large gaps in delivery times, this can be a wasteful expenditure for the retailer. This will affect the total cost of home delivery (Kämäräinen, 2001). To solve the inefficient problem, different solutions for goods receipts can be used. There are some existing examples from e-grocers, such as Streamline in the USA. Punakivi (2001) pointed out that the home delivery concept of Streamline is based on a reception box in the customer's garage or yard enabling unmanned reception. The use of reception boxes can cut delivery costs, and also take control of the delivery time window.

Another fairly large problem with home delivery is the issue of lost and stolen goods. Passers-by, neighbours witnessing the delivery or catching sight of the goods can easily steal them. Or goods may attract the driver's attention, which means the driver himself could steal the products. The customer can also exploit the absence of proof of delivery and fraudulently claim not to have received the goods. Customers cannot receive the product and the lack of proof of delivery may damage the relationship between customers and companies. Also, the presence of packages outside a house or building may increase the risk of theft when customers are not at home for the delivery time window. The couriers responsible for the delivery of items sometimes leave the products outside the consumer's property which is known as unsecured delivery. To deal with this kind of unsecured delivery, the reception boxes that are being used in the USA could be used to resolve the problem. The courier could also leave any products at another location for collection which customers can easily access. To make sure the delivery is delivered to the right person securely, expenditure of the retailer can again be a disadvantage.

Thirdly, home delivery could be costly. As mentioned before, the salary of staff and the cost of transportation could be a lot of money. Some companies do not have a delivery system but they have business need to depend on delivery, so they hire delivery companies to do the work. This can also cost a lot. As home delivery can be unsecured, the retailer must spend more to ensure security of products. Sometimes it is impossible to forecast the customer's demand, which is not good for the company to collect data and information to know what kinds of products are popular among the market and which step the supplier should take for next season or year.

10.4 In-store delivery

In more current times, operators try to combine different approaches to stock-keeping and picking and packing online orders with different models of delivering goods: home delivery, click and collect from store, and various delivery methods depending on the retailer. Among all the multichannel delivery methods, the concept of in-store delivery is very 'simple and counter-intuitive' (*The Telegraph*, 2013). The click and collect strategy enables customers to order their products online and then personally collect them from dedicated pick-up areas in stores (Pate & Adams, 2013).

Sainsbury's supermarket offered the service of click and collect to more than 800 shops during 2011, and almost 75% of online general merchandise orders were made via this channel. According to the user experience, click and collect is clearly signposted on product pages, integrating it effectively with other delivery options. A Sainsbury's Local, 0.4 miles from the selected postcode, was among the pick-up options, and there were four available locations within a mile, and 14 under 2 miles. In terms of communication, instant confirmation of the order was followed by a notification of delivery the next day – ahead of schedule. It also gave clear instructions of what documentation and ID to take to pick up the order. Customers will collect items by asking the staff to locate parcels. The inclusion of Local stores makes the service very convenient. Nevertheless, this service was only offered on groceries at the time of research (*Retail Week*, 2012).

Customers want and increasingly expect shorter lead times; flexibility, configurability, customisation; and things to work 'out of the box' (Dawson, 2002). In reference to this statement, retailers must compete with one another to ensure the best and most convenient service is offered to consumers as this will increase those likely to order from them. There are many advantages of in-store delivery for customers. For some consumers, in-store delivery is their preferred delivery service. Shopping convenience has been one of the principal motivations underlying customer inclination to adopt the choice of delivery methods (Beauchamp & Ponder, 2010; Colwell et al., 2008; Degeratu et al., 2000; Easterbrook, 1995; Lohse & Spiller, 1998; Moeller et al., 2009; Morganosky & Cude, 2000; Reimers & Clulow, 2009; Tanskanen et al., 2002).

120 Case study: an apparel delivery system

Two factors of primary importance in delivering convenient service to customers are time saving and effort minimisation (Etgar, 1978; Kotler & Zaltman, 1971; Seiders et al., 2000, 2005, 2007; Yale & Venkatesh, 1986). Convenience concerns psychological cost and other forms of non-monetary costs such as time, effort and stress (Aylott & Mitchell, 1998; Cassill et al., 1997). There are three main advantages of in-store delivery. First of all, in-store delivery can be extremely fast as customers can cut search and waiting time. Unlike previously, customers had to find their items of choice in their chosen retailer and queue to buy the items. The time-saving aspect of convenience has been intensively investigated in consumer waiting literature, particularly with respect to consumer reaction to waiting time (Gehrt & Yale, 1993).

The concept of effort saving refers to the minimisation of cognitive, physical and emotional activities that consumers must bear to purchase goods and services (Berry et al., 2002). Secondly, shipping costs of in-store delivery are often cheaper than home delivery or even waived. This is a win–win solution for both customers and retailers. Customers can save about £5 for each purchase. As Yan and Harmen (2006) mentioned, 'delivery charges by the online grocery retailers in the UK range from 0 (for large orders) to £5.99'. Thirdly, its customers can return unwanted items as easily as in real shops. The majority of brands that offer free returns have a link in the footer of the website and additional information about returns on the product page next to the product image. Brands need to ensure that they get across the message that returns are easy and don't require too much effort on the customers' side, by offering various convenient drop-off locations (*Experience Lab*, 2013).

On the other hand, there are three disadvantages to in-store delivery. First, it can be an inconvenience for consumers to travel to and from the physical store. 'Travel costs such as petrol or parking charges are clearly an expense as well' (Huang & Oppewal, 2006, p.67). Besides, if the online shopping is about clothes, customers are unable to try them on before making decisions. Second, it is very likely that customers will need to wait a long time in store. And in-store waiting times directly influence the whole customer experience. In Sainsbury's, customers have to wait for more than 15 minutes for packages because the employee could not find the reserved products. Sainsbury's click and collect service showed that they were not as prepared as expected in offering a flawless customer experience across channels (*Experience Lab*, 2013). Thirdly, some brands ask for the return of the item by post and payment of postage or for the product to be taken back to the same store from where the item was. These procedures might not be very convenient for the customer (*Experience Lab*, 2013).

At the same time, retailers want fewer inventories, less risk and greater reliability, as this means there is less damage so there will be fewer returns (Dawson, 2002). The superiorities of in-store delivery for retailers are comparatively more evident than for customers. Firstly, it sells a much broader product range online and gives customers more choice. Secondly, when customers are picking up their orders they often make additional unplanned purchases including products and services, which will increase the 'store traffic' and in turn will benefit the retailer. These two factors will help speed up merchandise turnover significantly. Thirdly, it improves online sales conversation rates and better customer services are offered through online conversation. Last but not least, no investment in reception technology is required.

Yet, there are still challenges. Attended reception (for example, home delivery) is the most common receiving concept today, which is why investment in reception technology is being acquired widely. Tight delivery windows and personal contact with the customer can extend delivery time detrimentally which also increases the expenditure of the retailer. Attended reception offers face-to-face service for customers who prefer this type of interaction. Also, customers tend to choose the nearest store to pick up from; however, if the store is out of stock, it needs extra transportation from another store or from the warehouse. This is time consuming and costs money.

10.5 Comparisons

The use of in-store delivery and home delivery share both similarities and a variety of differences. In-store delivery is mainly beneficial in comparison with home delivery as in-store delivery can cut costs for retailers. Compared with in-store delivery, many companies have to employ an additional courier service like Royal Mail to deliver their items, which can increase the expenditure of the company.

Due to the demand of needing more delivery providers, companies like Royal Mail and Yodel increased their prices which means if Sainsbury's were to introduce home delivery, this may cost them more initially due to the aforementioned increases in delivery costs from largely recognised low-cost couriers like Royal Mail. Additionally, the delivery services currently on offer for home delivery are competitive, with many companies offering free home delivery, which increased from 14% in 2011 to 17% in 2012.

Clarke et al. (2000) conducted a study which found that 46% of internet users stated free delivery of large orders as the key influence to encourage them to use an online grocery service in the future. However, in-store delivery has also been hugely popular with retailers and consumers for the low delivery cost. In-store delivery has led to an increase in sales in many large retailers such as John Lewis, which stated that their click and collect in-store delivery service represented 30%–35% of their online orders and had increased by 57% since 2013. As a result of these factors, economically in-store delivery may be favoured by the retailer and consumer.

One large disadvantage of home delivery is unsecured delivery. McKinnon and Tallam (2002) pointed out that theft could occur at several points along the home delivery channel. The term unsecured delivery gives reference to the delivery of an item to a customer's home address that they do not directly receive. Courier services may leave the item with a neighbour, in a bin or 'safe place', but due to this, many items are lost or damaged. This can occur through passers-by and neighbours

122 Case study: an apparel delivery system

witnessing an unsecured delivery and intercepting the parcel before the consumer receives it. As a result of consumers never receiving their parcels, many consumers ask for a refund or replacement and so the retailers are often inclined to oblige, once again running up costs. With an in-store delivery service in place, this is much less likely to be an issue as there is a clear tracking service by reference number and by the consumer's name. Additionally, the problem of the lost or damaged items can be rectified at the time as customers will be picking up an item from an employee of the store so they experience a level of customer service which is absent with home delivery.

However, due to retailers' experience of unsecured delivery, they have started to implement more secure methods of delivery. There are new ways of secure delivery including 'collect+' delivery, whereby items are delivered to nearby locations as part of a scheme like newsagents and petrol stations. This further provides convenience for those having their items delivered to their home as the 'collect+' locations are largely open until late evening so parcels can be easily collected if the consumer works. This also contributes to the security of the product.

There are advantages of home delivery, the most prevalent being the convenience element. It is much more convenient for a consumer to order their desired product to their home without having to go to a store to find the item. Smaros et al. (2000) found that grocers like Sainsbury's have to shift from trading physical goods alone, to providing services for customers, to achieve profit growth. Therefore, the development of home delivery will be of much benefit to Sainsbury's as it provides a convenience for those who cannot visit a store for in-store delivery.

However, in-store delivery can be a more convenient delivery option for some consumers; if they live near to the branch or if they are already going to the branch to shop. To ensure the customers are not inconvenienced, many retailers send a text message or email to confirm when an item has been delivered to the store. This is beneficial for both the consumer and the retailer as it means the product is easily categorised and readily available for collection. This also means that due to the clear organisation, pick-up time is cut short and customers are more likely to be happy with the service, encouraging them to purchase again via in-store delivery.

10.6 Summary

After researching into Sainsbury's supply chain, it was found that Sainsbury's does not have a delivery system in place for online orders of their Tu clothing brand to be delivered. After finding the initial problem, we also found issues surrounding the problem which needed to be considered when finding solutions for the problem. In order to overcome the problem two solutions were found; these were found after looking at what competitors are currently offering and what the demand is in this current market. The two solutions that were found were in-store delivery and home delivery. A detailed analysis was conducted on both solutions to help show how well the solutions would work. The analysis included a comparison of the advantages and disadvantages which helped to confirm which solution would overcome the problem more easily. It was found that in-store delivery would be the best option on a trial basis as you can see from the points that have been made; it is a cheaper alternative with the option of being very successful giving both the customer and Sainsbury's satisfaction. On the basis of the in-store delivery being successful, investing in home delivery would be a good idea as it could help to draw in a new market of customers.

Note

1 This research was carried out in 2015 as an individual research project.

References

Alba, J. & Lynch, J. (1997). *Interactive Home Shopping: Consumer, Retailer, and Manufacturer Incentives to Participate in Electronic Marketplaces.* Available at: http://web.a.ebscohost.com/ ehost/detail?sid=da96d749-0ad5-4682-90f8 372c0a6def80%40sessionmgr4001&vid=1& hid=4106&bdata=JkF1dGhUeXBlPWlwLHNoaWImc2l0ZT1laG9zdC1s aXZl [accessed 2 May 2017].

Aylott, R. & Mitchell, V.-W. (1998). An exploratory study of grocery shopping stressors. *International Journal of Retail & Distribution Management*, 26(9), pp. 362–373.

Bearne, S. (2013). Business delivery: Logistics. *Drapers.* Available at: www.drapersonline. com/in-business/business-delivery logistics/5049392.article#.U2Np8_ldViN [accessed 2 May 2018].

Beauchamp, M.B. & Ponder, N. (2010). Perceptions of retail convenience for in-store and online shoppers. *The Marketing Management Journal*, 20(1), pp. 49–65.

Berry, L.L., Seiders, K. & Grewal, D. (2002). Understanding service convenience. *Journal of Marketing*, 66(3), pp. 1–7.

Beth, B. (2013). Available at: www.thegrocer.co.uk/companies/supermarkets/ sainsburys/sa insburys-daventry-distribution-centre-to-open-in-2015/351758.article [accessed 24 April 2018].

Boyer, K.K., Hult, G.T. & Frohlich, M. (2003). An exploratory analysis of extended grocery supply chain operations and home delivery. *Integrated Manufacturing Systems*, 14(8), pp. 652–663.

Brooks, A. (2013). Stretching global production networks: The international second-hand clothing trade. *Geoforum*, 44, January, pp. 10–22.

Browne, M. & Gomez, M. (2011). The impact on urban distribution operations of upstream supply chain constraints. *International Journal of Physical Distribution & Logistics Management*, 31(9), pp. 896–912.

Bryant, N.O., Burns, L.D. & Mullet, K.K. (2012). *The Business of Fashion Designing, Manufacturing, and Marketing.* US: Bloomsbury Academic.

Case Studies (n.d.). *Sainsbury's cuts transport costs with integrated paragon system.* Available at: www.paragonrouting.com/uk/case-studies/sainsbury-s-cuts-transport-costs-with-integra ted-paragon-system.

Cassill, N.L., Thomas, J.B. & Bailey, E.M. (1997). Consumers' definitions of apparel value: An investigation of department store shoppers. *Journal of Fashion Marketing and Management: An International Journal*, 1(4), pp. 308–321.

Catherine, N. (2013a). Tesco clothing hits £1bn as group profits fall. *Drapers*. Available at: www.drapersonline.com/news/tesco-clothing-hits-1bn-as-group-profits-fall/5048292.arti cle#.U1JxuBYbxhA [accessed 14 April 2018].

Catherine, N. (2013b). Sainsbury's menswear arm rises 23% as top line sales fall. *Drapers*. Available at: www.drapersonline.com/news/sainsburys-menswear-arm-rises-23-as-top -line-sales-fall/5058427.article [accessed 2 May 2018].

Chen, Mu-Chen, Chang, Kuo-Chien, Hsu, Chia-Lin & Yang, I-Ching (1989). Under-standing the relationship between service convenience and customer satisfaction in home delivery by Kano model. *Asia Pacific Journal of Marketing & Logistics*. Available at: www.em eraldinsight.com/journals.htm?issn=1355-5855&volume=23&issue=3&articleid= 1938038&show=html [accessed 2 May 2018].

Clarke, I., Dodd, C.A., Baron, S. & Houston, V. (2000). Practitioner Papers: 'Looking the part': Identity, meaning and culture in clothing purchasing – Theoretical considerations. *Journal of Fashion Marketing and Management: An International Journal*, 4.

Clements, A. (2012). Putting a Price on Deliveries. *Drapers*. Available at: www.draperson line.com/in-business/features/putting-a-price-on-deliveries/5036998.article#.U2Nvq_ ldViO [accessed 2 May 2014].

Colla, E. & Lapoule, P. (2012). E-commerce: Exploring the critical success factors. *International Journal of Retail & Distribution Management*, 40(11), pp. 842–864.

Colwell, S.R., Aung, M., Kanetkar, V. & Holder, A.L. (2008). Toward a measure of service convenience: Multiple-item scale development and empirical test. *Journal of Services Marketing*, 22(2), pp. 160–169.

Davey, J. (2013). Sainsbury's seven percent profit rise puts Tesco in shade. Reuters. Available at: http://uk.reuters.com/article/2013/11/13/uk-sa insbury-results-idUKBRE9AC07L20131113.

Dawson, A. (2002). Supply Chain technology. *Work Study*, 51(4), pp. 191–196. Available at: www.duluth.umn.edu/~hrallis/guides/researching/litreview.html.

Degeratu, A.M., Rangaswamy, A. & Wu, J.N. (2000). Consumer choice behavior in online and traditional supermarkets: The effects of brand name, price, and other search attributes. *International Journal of Research in Marketing*, 17, pp. 55–78.

Durand, B. & Senkel, M.P. (2007). La logistique de l'epicerie en ligne: vers une differ-enciation des solutions. *Decisions Marketing*, 45, pp. 75–89.

Easterbrook, G. (1995). *A Moment on the Earth: The Coming of Age of Environmental Optimism*. New York, NY: Viking Press.

Etgar, M. (1978). Selection of an effective channel control mix. *Journal of Marketing*, 42, July, pp. 53–57.

Experience Lab (2013). Click&Collect Customer Experience. Available at: www.serco.com/ Images/Click%26Collect%203MB_tcm3-40383.pdf.

Fernie, J., Sparks, L. & McKinnon, A.C. (2010). Retail logistics in the UK: Past, present and future. *International Journal of Retail & Distribution Management*, 38(11/12), pp. 894–914.

Gehrt, K.C. & Yale, L.J. (1993). The dimensionality of the convenience phenomenon: A qualitative reexamination. *Journal of Business and Psychology*, 18(2), pp. 163–180.

Huang, Y. & Oppewal, H. (2006). Why consumers hesitate to shop online: An experi-mental choice analysis of grocery shopping and the role of delivery fees. *International Journal of Retail & Distribution Management*, 34(4/5), pp. 334–353.

Jiang, L.A., Yang, Z. & Jun, M. (2013). Measuring Consumer Perceptions of Online Shopping Convenience. *Journal of Service Management*, 24(2), pp. 191–214.

Kämäräinen, V., Saranen, J. & Holmström, J. (2001). The reception box impact on home delivery efficiency in the e-grocery business. *International Journal of Physical Distribution & Logistics Management*, 31(6), pp. 414–426.

Kirklees Business News (2013). 18 June, p. 2.

Kotler, P. & Zaltman, G. (1971). Social marketing an approach to planned social change. *Journal of Marketing*, 35, pp. 3–12.

Lohse, G.L. & Spiller, P. (1998). Electrical shopping. *Communications of the ACM*, 41(7), pp. 81–87.

McKinnon, A.C. & Tallam, D. (2002). *New Crime Threats from e-Tailing: Theft in the Home Delivery Channel, report prepared for the Crime Panel of the UK Government Foresight Programme.* London: Department of Trade and Industry. Available at: www.foresight.gov.uk.

McKinnon, A.G. & Tallam, D. (2003). Unattended delivery to the home: An assessment of the security implications. *International Journal of Retail & Distribution Management*, 31(1), pp. 30–41.

Moeller, S., Fassnacht, M. & Ettinger, A. (2009). Retaining customers with shopping convenience. *Journal of Relationship Marketing*, 8, pp. 313–329.

Morganosky, M.A. & Cude, B.J. (2000). Attention retailers how convenient is your convenience strategy? *International Journal of Retail & Distribution Management*, 37(7), pp. 541–562.

n.a. (2002). The e-tailing delivery conundrum. *Strategic Direction*, 18(1), pp. 14–16. Available at: www.emeraldinsight.com/journals.htm?issn=02580543&volume=18&issue=1&articleid=869196&show=html [accessed 2 May 2018].

Neilan, C. (2013). White Stuff hires Superdrug boss as chief executive. *Drapers*, p. 1.

Neilan, C. (2014). How do the UK's supermarket shoppers look? *Cityam.com*.

Nielsen (2011). *Croissance: le e-commerce*, March. Paris: Rencontre Nielsen.

Oliver, M. (2013). *David Jones strives to boost online revenue and in-store traffic with new 'click and collect' service.* Available at: www.smartcompany.com.au/growth/economy/33325-david-jones-strives-to-boost-online-revenue-and-in-store-traffic-with-new–click-and-collect–service.html.

Pate, S.S. & Adams, M. (2013). The Influence of Social Networking Sites on Buying Behaviors of Millennials. *Atlantic Marketing Journal*, 2(1), article 7. Available at: https://digitalcommons.kennesaw.edu/amj/vol2/iss1/7.

Punakivi, M. & Saranen, P.J. (2001). Identifying the success factors in e-grocery home delivery. *International Journal of Retail & Distribution Management*, 29(4), pp. 156–163.

Punakivi, M. & Taskanen, K. (2002). Increasing the cost efficiency of e-fulfillment using shared reception boxes. *International Journal of Retail & Distribution Management*, 30(10), pp. 498–507.

Punakivi, M., Yrjölö, H. & Holmstöm, J. (2001). Solving the last mile issue: Reception box or delivery box? *International Journal of Physical Distribution & Logistic Management*, 31(6), pp. 427–439.

Reimers, V. & Clulow, V. (2009). Retail centres: It's time to make them convenient. *International Journal of Retail & Distribution Management*, 37(7), pp. 541–562.

Retail Week (2012). Highs and lows of click-and-collect. Available at: www.retail-week.com/multichannel/highs-and-lows-of-click-and-collect/ 5037714.article.

Seiders, K., Berry, L.L. & Gresham, L. (2000). Attention retailers: How convenient is your convenience strategy? *Sloan Management Review*, 49(3), pp. 79–90.

Seiders, K., Voss, G.B., Godfrey, A.L. & Grewal, D. (2007). SERVCON: Development and validation of a multidimensional service convenience scale. *Journal of the Academy Marketing Science*, 35, pp. 144–156.

Seiders, K., Voss, G.B., Grewal, D. & Godfrey, A.L. (2005). Do satisfied customers buy more? Examining moderating influences in a retailing context. *Journal of the Academy Marketing Science*, 35, pp. 144–156.

Smaros, J., Holmstrom, J. & Kamarainen, V. (2000). New service opportunities in the e-grocery business. *International Journal of Logistics Management*, 11(1), pp. 61–74.

126 Case study: an apparel delivery system

Tanskanen, K., Yrjola, H. & Holmstrom, J. (2002). The way to profitable internet grocery retailing – six lessons learned. *International Journal of Retail & Distribution Management*, 30 (4), pp. 169–178.

The Telegraph (2013). Click and Collect – the new way to go shopping. Available at: www.telegraph.co.uk/finance/newsbysector/retailandconsumer/9785532/Click-and-collect-the-new-way-to-go-shopping.html.

Yale, L. & Venkatesh, A. (1986). Toward the Construct of Convenience in Consumer Research. *Advances in Consumer Research*, 13, pp. 403–408.

Yan, H. & Harmen, O. (2006). Why consumers hesitate to shop online: An experimental choice analysis of grocery shopping and the role of delivery fees. *International Journal of Retail & Distribution Management*, 34(4/5), pp. 334–353.

INDEX

age, in fashion market 19–20
agile supply chain: advantages of 32–34, **33**; capitalisation with 34; customisation and 32; disadvantages of 32–34, **33**; flexibility in 33; lean supply chain and **37**, 37–39; postponement and 31–32; volatility and 31; worker skills and 33
alternative evaluation 24
anonymity 95–96

barcodes *55*, 55–56, 59–61, **60**
behaviour *see* consumer behaviour
blogs 91–96
brand image building 98–99
brand use practice 92
build-to order (BTO) supply chain **5**

capitalisation: in agile supply chain 34
China 17–18
click and collect 115
closed-loop system, in supply chain traceability 61–62
collectivism 21, 22
communication, data from 80
competitive advantage 29
complementarity 83
consumer behaviour: consumer characteristics in 70–71; culture influence on 20; defined 65; factors in 65–66; hedonism and 68; impulse 66–68; product characteristics in 69; supply chain traceability and 58
consumer confidence 9

consumer decision-making 23–25
consumer demand 1
consumer needs, identification of 16–17
copyright protection 99
cost structure 9
cultural dimension 20–23
culture: fashion, evolution of 18–19; influence of 20; popular, proliferation of 29
customer responsiveness 36
customisation 32

data: from communication 80–81; from observation 80–81; primary 80–81; secondary 79–80; transactional 84
data analysis 84–85
data collection: method 83–84; mixed 82–83; qualitiative 81–82; quantitative 81
data sources 79–81
decsion-making, by consumers 23–25
delivery system 115–123
demand 1
development, in data collection 83

efficiency: in lean supply chain 36
effort saving 120
environment, supply chain 4
epistemology 76
ethical consumers 8
expansion, in data collection 83

fashion: characteristics 16; in China 17–18; concepts of 18–20; culture, evolution of 18–19; defined 16–18; industry 17

128 Index

fashion blogging 92–96
fast fashion 6–7, 18–19, 96–97
femininity 22
flexibility 33, 38–39
France 18
functional needs 16–17

globalisation 46, 109, 111
global supply chain risk 105–106; *see also* supply chain risk management

haute couture 18
hedonism 68
Hofstede's cultural dimension theories 20–21
home delivery 117–119, 121–122
horizontal integration 49; *see also* supply chain integration

identity: social media and 94–95
impulse purchasing behaviour 66–68; *see also* consumer behaviour
India 5
individualism 21, 22
information search 23–24
initiation, in data collection 83
in-store delivery 119–121
integration, supply chain *see* supply chain integration
intellectual property 99
interpretivism 77

just-in-time (JIT) supply chain **5**, 34, 35, 36–37; *see also* lean supply chain

lead times 119
lean supply chain: advantages of **35**, 35–37; agile supply chain and **37**, 37–39; customer responsiveness and 36; defined 34; disadvantages of **35**, 35–37; efficiency of 36; risk management and 108; supply shocks and 36–37; training and 36
life cycles, product 29
long-term orientation 22
luxury fashion: social media and 96, 97–98

masculinity 22

needs, consumer 16–17

observation, as data source 80–81
off-shoring 4–6, **5**
ontology 76
open-loop system, in supply chain traceability 61–62

operational risk drivers 108
outsourcing 4–6, **5**

popular culture, proliferation of 29
positivism 76–77
postponement supply chain **5**, 31–32
post-purchase evaluation 24–25
power distance 21
pragmatism 77–78
primary data 80–81
proble recognition 23
product characteristics, in consumer behaviour 69
product life cycles 29
purchase decision 24

QR codes 56
qualitative data collection 81–82
quantitative data collection 81

radio frequency identification (RFID) 54, 56–59, *57*, 59–61, **60**, 61–62
ready-to-wear 18
realism 77
research approach 78
research methodology(ies): data analysis in 84–85; data collection in 81–84; data sources in 79–81; defined 75; epistemology in 76; interpretivism in 77; ontology in 76; positivism in 76–77; pragmatism in 77–78; realism in 77; sampling in 85–86; validation in 85–86
research philosophy 76–78
responsivness: customer 36; of supply chain 30
RFID *see* radio frequency identification (RFID)
risk drivers 107–108
risk management *see* supply chain risk management

Sainsbury's 115–123
sampling 85–86
SCM *see* supply chain management (SCM)
SCRM *see* supply chain risk management (SCRM)
SCT *see* supply chain transparency (SCT)
secondary data 79–80
self-creation 95
self-identity 8–9
short-term orientation 22
social media: anonymity and 95–96; blogs in 91–96; brand image building and 98–99; brand use practice and 92; defined 90; fashion industry and 91–92; fashion

markets and 96–98; fast fashion and 96–97; identity and 94–95; influence of 91; luxury fashion and 96, 97–98; self-creation and 95

stolen goods, home delivery and 118

supply chain: build-to order **5**; customer-driven **5**; definitions of **2**; environment 4; just-in-time **5**, 34, 35, 36–37; postponement **5**, 31–32; responsiveness of 30; and supply chain management 2–3, **3**; traceability 54–63, *55*, *57*, **60**; volatility in 29–31; *see also* agile supply chain; lean supply chain

supply chain integration: in apparel industry 46–47; globalisation and 46; horizontal 49; literature review on 45–46; vertical 47–48; vertical *vs.* horizontal 49–50

supply chain management (SCM): definitions of **3**; supply chain and 2–3, **3**

supply chain risk management (SCRM): defined 104; framework for 109–110; globalisation and 109, 111; and global supply chain risk 105–106; importance of 106–107; proactive 108; reactive 108; risk drivers in 107–108

supply chain transparency (SCT) 7–8

supply shocks: lean supply chain and 36–37

sustainability 7–9

teenagers 19–20

template analysis 85

theft, and home delivery 118

Toyota 34

traceability, supply chain 54–63, *55*, *57*, **60**

training: lean supply chain and 36

transactional data 84

transparency *see* supply chain transparency (SCT)

triangulation 83

uncertainty avoidance 21–22

United Kingdom: fashion market in 17

unsecured delivery 121–122

validation, in research 85–86

vertical integration 47–48; *see also* supply chain integration

volatility 29–31, 38

wages, outsourcing and 6

willingness to pay (WTP): ethical consumers and 8

WTP *see* willingness to pay (WTP)

youth 19–20

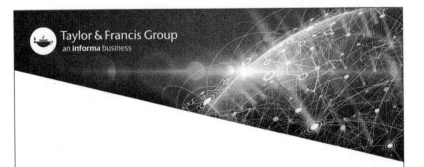